8.2004

Don't Well

Dear Carle

Sister — you
are always
in
my
heart!
Love
Garth

This Life
and the *Fireworks*

Carole Dale

authorHOUSE®

AuthorHouse™
1663 Liberty Drive
Bloomington, IN 47403
www.authorhouse.com
Phone: 1-800-839-8640

First published by AuthorHouse 6/19/2009

ISBN: 978-1-4389-9563-2 (sc)

Cover concept: Gay Walker Dale
Staging: Carole Dale
Photographer: James Muha

Printed in the United States of America
Bloomington, Indiana

This book is printed on acid-free paper.

This Life
and the *Fireworks*

Short, true stories to be savored like cupcakes; each bite filled with vivid descriptions and unique experiences. All recalled and told by the narrator through the prisms of her memory.

By CAROLE DALE

AWARDS FOR MAJOR SUPPORTING ROLES:

I must acknowledge these wonderful individuals who have believed in me and offered their selfless commitment to my achieving the dream of writing this book, *This Life and the Fireworks.*

It has taken most of my life to realize how much I love to write—in school I was thrilled when my essay or poem was selected to be read to the class. My head never swelled with pride, but my heart overflowed with gratitude. I loved that someone else could find meaning in my words.

The first award goes to Dr. Stephen F. Dale. He bought books to explain grammar and punctuation but never held it against me that I was incapable of understanding either. He never tried to interrupt my organic method of writing. Stephen has and continues to believe in me, and it has made all the difference in my life. Aunt Lee Lee would say when I entered the room, "Here comes nothing!" She said it with affection, but I did fear that she might be right. Stephen has helped me to believe otherwise.

Career took much of my writing energy—writing was for proposals to raise money for my programs, memoranda, etc. It has only been after retiring that I could write for myself. Perhaps these recollections could not appear on the horizon of my memory earlier because there was no room!

When the cupcakes began coming through me the first person to hear them has been my friend Joseph Sarah. He is a mean wordsmith and through arguments and humor has been crucial to the cupcake production. I usually read them over the phone to him. He hates to be read to but for some amazing test of patience has listened to all of them, and I thank him for the ear time and his excellent corrections and many good suggestions. He said one day that I write as if "Faulkner had married Gertrude Stein." Trust me, this was not a compliment!

The major reason the cupcakes have gone public is because of a dynamo who is barely five feet tall but casts a long shadow, Dr. Katherine Burkman. She invited me to join her merry band of "Women at Play" who for twelve years wrote plays and performed to a loyal following. Although we have retired that group, some of us have now formed "Wild Women Writing!" (WWW).

This wild band of seven serious women of the pen consists of the following: Pat Ake, who I am sure was my mother in another life because of her unconditional commitment to all things Carole. Pat dedicates her life to teaching others the power of self-expression by writing in a journal every day. Pat blends the analytical with the essence of all things, and we love her contributions to our group.

Anne Brethauer, who is so smart she sparkles and who can in one sentence create plot, intrigue, and scene descriptions from which Stephen Spielberg could make an Oscar-winning movie.

Dr. Ann Hall, who has a Triscuit cracker fetish and can scare your hair off with her insights into the complexities of human relations that encompass terror and humor simultaneously and takes our breath away.

Susie Gerald, who reveals all the foibles of being female in hilarious first person. Her candor allows the reader to live vicariously through her bravery and helps us all look into the mirror with more honesty.

Our magazine journalist, Laura Zakin, who captures every detail of a story and transports the reader into time, plot, and place with the precision of a brain surgeon.

And the aforementioned Kathy Burkman, our taskmaster, who by the stroke of her keys can become a convincing six years old, have an affair with a gambling machine, or be a figure of mystery and intrigue in her stories.

Can you feel the great energy! We meet every other Thursday and do public performances of our pieces.

These fabulous writers have insisted that my cupcakes are book worthy and have cheered me on with their critiques and enthusiasm. Katherine has nipped at my heels and risen on her toes to a full five feet to lower her glasses and demand, Lucy style, "Get it published!" But most importantly she edited the entire manuscript, every last page her sharp eyes surveyed. "She who must be obeyed" is a jewel!

To my circle sisters, Monica Brown, Leslie DelGigante, Nancy Evans, Mary Finke, Marianne Gerth, Becky Lowther, Barbara Mickler, and Ruth Siegle, for cheering me on I offer my love and thanks. Who says two Catholics, three Jews, one Buddhist, one Agnostic, one Mennonite, and one failed Episcopalian can't seek spiritual growth through mutual explorations and deep personal commitment to sisterhood? No, we are not a cult!

Ruth Siegle, who always gets a special look in her eyes and says, "That was wonderful," after I read one of my cupcakes to her—she, a wonderful poet and photographer, inspires me. She and Becky Lowther shared the rocky road with me of writing and producing "Lasting Impressions," a history of the Columbus Museum of Art Docent Program, and it is a special bond that will never be erased. We would march into fire for each other I am sure.

My wonderful long-time friends the Magnolias, Grace Franklin, Lisa Holstein, and Kathy Watt, who always enjoyed hearing the cupcakes and supported my writing. We had great fun and anxious moments handling heads of state and VIPs who visited The Ohio State University. Lots of memories! Remember Henry Kissinger? Thank you! A little help from my friends has made all the difference.

For sweet friends who would ask me to read cupcakes at their dinner parties, it was very flattering to be asked, and I loved doing it. I send my gratitude across the ocean to my Bavarian prince, Christian Simmler, for paying international telephone rates to hear a cupcake.

A very special bow to Miss Kitty, who assisted in every way a cat can. Most impressive, her willingness to offer herself as resistance training in lieu of my going to the gym by sitting on top of my wrists while typing. She added drama by walking on the keys and making things happen that I was clueless to undo. Thanks to Dr. Mac, Jim Muha, who cheerfully undid her footwork and programmed my manuscript with technical knowhow that would have driven me mad!

Finally, I thank the beautiful Mary Finke, my circle sister, for reading with "cold eyes" the final manuscript and catching many typos and other mistakes I had made. The British Eagle, our nickname for her, has a keen ability to spot errors that borders on the uncanny! Mary reassured me that given the peculiar pastiche of individual stories told here they still work together, in her opinion, to make a good book. Bless you Mary for those words!

I remember how affected I was by the song "You'll Never Walk Alone" when I graduated from high school, and I must say what a happy life it is when this is true.

"And when the Sage entered Nirvana, the Earth quivered like a ship struck by a squall, and firebrands fell from the sky. The heavens were lit up by a preternatural fire. Beautiful flowers that grew out of season on the trees bent down and showered his golden body with their flowers."

Birth, Defeat of the Devil, First Sermon, Entry into Nirvana. From a manuscript of the Perfection of Wisdom, India (Bihar), 11th century.

The Cupcake Menu

Fire as Metaphor

People who have consumed my "Legible Cupcakes" that fill the pages of this book often ask, "Why the title 'This Life and the Fireworks'? This phrase comes from the lips of my mother; to my knowledge it is original. When Mother would utter this phrase she always rolled her eyes and shook her head to punctuate the drama. It seems a perfect summation and a perfect metaphor for both our lives!

The recognition that fire has recurred and burned memorable events throughout my life suddenly flashed through my mind. It began when I was growing up by the DuPont factory in Lower Belle, West Virginia. At that time the coke ovens, a half block from our house, opened their fiery jaws every evening, casting the reflection of orange and red flames in a dance across my bedroom walls. It was strange to recite my little child's prayer, "Now I lay me down to sleep. I pray the Lord my soul to keep. If I should die before I wake, I pray the Lord my soul to take," surrounded by what felt like hell's fire. I always expected to be burned alive!

I was nineteen when a fire destroyed our family possessions, all the photographs, my high school yearbook, everything gone, burned. Only my piano survived because as fate interceded I had happened to give it to a young girl a week before the fire.

In the middle of a cold February night a harsh knocking came at the front door. It was a fireman warning me that the gasoline station on the corner was on fire and the entire block might explode. I needed to evacuate immediately. I remember snatching my young son, Rob, from his crib, wrapping him in his satin "puff," as he called his blanket, throwing on my winter coat, and racing out the door. I had very long black hair, and the wind was blowing it fiercely around my face. I could barely see to run down the street. Sparks of fire were falling like rain, and I kept thinking my hair was going to catch fire. I must not drop Rob! After running for a couple of blocks I became curious that Rob was completely quiet. I wondered, could he be sleeping through this nightmare? I stopped and turned to see the night sky filled with flames. It was a frightening sight, but more striking was the expression on my son's face. His little eyes were wide open and mesmerized. He looked like he was in a trance. At that instant I wondered, "Oh my God, will this child be a fireman or a pyromaniac!"

When my only sibling, my baby brother Scotty, was dying from lung cancer and the side effects of Agent Orange, I drove to Florida to be with him, and fire was on both sides of the highway. It was January and Florida was in flames! When I reached his home in Palm Bay, clouds of smoke were encroaching. I could feel so vividly that fire had come to lift him away. He and I began in a fiery room as children, and now I would be with him as he crossed over into the other side of life; fire and smoke and cremation were to be witnesses to my grief.

Each of the cupcakes was written and conceived as a performance piece to be read aloud and was not originally planned to be in a book. This idea came later as people requested having them together in a collection. For this reason you are not going to have a continuous narrative, but instead each cupcake will stand on its own merits connected by the common theme of this writer's life.

I have many cupcakes yet to be written ("if the good Lord is willing and the creeks don't rise," as my mother would say), other fires to describe, and as they insist on coming to me I shall obey. I hope you enjoy reading these cupcakes and each bite will leave you with a good taste and wanting more.

Carole Elaine Stewart Dale

PS: Rob, my son, has been a fireman for twenty years and has never wanted to be anything else. He is a hero, a wonderful husband to his wife Debbie and father to three sons, Robby Gene, Aaron, and Joshua. He hopes someday one of the boys will be a fireman, but "no pressure!"

My Arrival

I arise lily white from the fertile Ohio River mud. My Pomeroy mother bore me on a perfect autumn afternoon at four o'clock on my grandmother's dining room table where angel food cake and coffee are usually laid.

Mamma could swim across the Ohio River and was a member of a secret club called the River Rats. The Ohio River had been pretty much the center of her life until she fell in love with my father.

Pomeroy, Ohio, has always been a mistress to the Ohio River. The river brought excitement to the town; in summer, party boats would stop at the levee and my mother and her sisters would go on evening cruises and dance under the warm summer moon. In the spring the careless river would fling its blanket of high water and the town would go under. My mother grew up understanding that nature has its way with your life and it's best to just accept who has the upper hand.

My father, who was from Racine, a nearby river town, chauffeured the local doctor on his rounds. The Doc usually had a little too much of the local moonshine in his system to be driving himself. The point is it brought Dad to Pomeroy where he met the delightful Edith Mae. He had already graduated from high school, but Mamma had another year before she would finish. She made excellent grades and was the acknowledged star of the senior class play.

Edie Mae lost her father when she was four years old. Theodore had died in a mining accident; his body was laid out in the house on Cave Street in Monkey Run, the German-speaking part of Pomeroy. I was told by my grandmother that he didn't have a mark on his body; he didn't look hurt, just handsome—he was just thirty-five. Mama's baby sister was born four months after her father's death and given his name, Theodore. Seven children were left with no pension to support them. My grandmother held her family together and turned down offers from well-meaning neighbors who particularly wanted to adopt my mother. Why Mama? She was the youngest of the children when her father died. Perhaps her golden ringlets, sapphire blue eyes, and outstanding sweet disposition made her especially appealing.

The two-mile walk to school in the winter could be brutal between the wind off the river, the snow, and the cold temperatures. My father saw that my mother didn't have a proper coat to keep her warm, and one of the first things he did to show his love was to buy her a winter coat. The coat symbolized protection and a warm embrace and perhaps explains why she always referred to my father as "Daddy."

My parents were married in Parkersburg, on the Ohio River, in 1936, and the portrait of my mother on her wedding day shows a lovely young woman, 1930s movie star worthy, who I imagine believed her happy fate had just begun.

Life's Lottery

I am here to tell the story of *This Life and the Fireworks* only because a young man in a faraway country did not follow the destiny his parents had planned, which was that Matthias Martin Sauer, their second son, should become a Catholic priest in their village of Oppau in Bavaria, Germany. Matthias strongly felt a different calling, so he ran away and boarded a ship bound for the United States of America. During the crossing he fell in love and married a Bavarian girl named Anna Maria Findling. Their destiny is the seed of my mother's family. Matthias and Anna Maria settled down in the Ohio River town of Pomeroy, which offered both a German-speaking community and work on the river. Matthias's love for the Danube in Germany was now given to the rough and mighty Ohio River, which represented everything he had sought, the freedom and challenge in this new land called America.

Matthias joined the West Virginia militia during the Civil War as a union soldier, surviving forty-five major battles without a scratch, including having three horses shot out from under him.

In 1882 their daughter Maria married Jacob E. Fischer of Pomeroy and gave birth to my mother's father, Theodore Fischer, in 1883. As a young man seeking work he later moved to Campbell's Creek, West Virginia, to labor in the mines. He stayed in a boarding house owned by John and Emeline Shannon, where he met and married their daughter, my grandmother, Bessie Shannon, in 1906.

In other words, life is a chess game and the players before us set the stage for the lives to follow. This is how my mother arrived, through the joining of Bessie and Theodore; she, the sixth child, was born in 1916. When my mother's father was tragically killed in a mining accident in 1920, her mother Bessie was pregnant with their seventh child. Four months after her father's death, Aunt Teddy was born, and the story told is that my grandmother, "Mom," the midwife in Monkey Run, ended up delivering this last child herself because no one could come quickly enough to help.

Well, how many of us have delivered our own children? This tall, large-boned, gentle woman with soft bluebell eyes seemed possessed of extraordinary energy and ability. There was no pension for widows at that time, and Mom was determined to keep her family together. She later agreed to marry an older bachelor named George Enzensauer for his pension. He basically moved into her home for bed and board.

Daily life was forever changed. My grandfather Theodore had wanted all his children to learn a musical instrument and to be well educated. An elder daughter, Freda, already played the piano and violin, but the reality of day-to-day existence now removed these aspirations from the younger children.

My grandmother, "Mom" as we called her, planted large gardens in the rich soil of Pomeroy and grew all of their food. She planted orchards on the property and raised chickens at the bottom of the hill. She took in laundry and baked bread. My mother said Mom also made their underwear from flour sacks, and all the clothes were recycled down the ages of the kids. Being next to the youngest, she really felt she was at the end of the line. As if George and seven children were not enough, my grandmother also took in her sisters Lil and Min. Lil was mad as two hatters and mostly rocked in the front porch swing thinking and plotting how to get her next piece of Black Jack chewing gum. I remember that as very young children my brother and I came to visit on Easter weekend. Sunday morning when we searched for our Easter baskets with colored eggs and candy, neither was to be found. For the first time I saw my grandmother be firm with her sister, "Lil, where did you put the children's Easter candy?" Slowly, with no shred of remorse, she led us into her bedroom where all the Easter goodies lay hidden in a drawer with her underwear.

Mom and her sister Min competed to do the chores. Min would sneak into her sister's room at night to see what time she had set her alarm and would set her own clock an hour earlier. Mom won by outliving Mim who died from a heart attack after climbing a ladder. For these Pomeroy women home and hearth were everything and I am so grateful to share their blood.

The Dream

I never know when the dream will return, but I am back on Cave Street in Monkey Run in Pomeroy in my grandmother's home. Built on a steep hill, the white house rests diagonally but with *Alice in Wonderland* magic; you open the iron gate and the garden walk is flat and symmetrical, one side dropping off a stone wall and the other stone wall holding the hill at bay.

Mom's white roses are planted in straight rows on either side; the foxglove and Queen Anne's lace add color and energy to the garden. When you reach the front porch, the scent of roses gives way to the aroma of Murphy's Oil Soap. Mom constantly scrubbed everything! The porch swing faced downhill to the main artery of Monkey Run, with Miner's grocery store just below the lip of the ash dump that drops thirty-five feet to meet the bank of the Ohio River.

I open the front door and my memory reconstructs everything as it was; the piano in the corner, the curio cabinet with the oriental teacups, so translucent you see through them when you hold the cup to your lips. The sofa rests against the wall on which there is a large painting of a winter river scene with heavy snow and steam rising from the water. I see the lace curtains, the large reading chair, a writing desk, and the iron stove to heat the upstairs.

I hurry down the stairs to the kitchen where Mom is baking her bread. The smell is heaven sent; it is too perfect for earthly life. All her children, Marcella, Mildred, Freda, Richard, Carl, Edith, and Theodore (and later we grandchildren), crowd into the kitchen and wait for the religious experience of eating the hot bread from the oven with Mom's home- churned butter. I wonder if God counted how many loaves of bread she made in her lifetime and how many people she nourished. Only my mother carried on the bread-baking tradition. My father never ate store-bought bread in his twenty-five years with my mother.

As I wander from room to room, warm memories wash over me. The bathroom is where my aunts would gather for girl talk. My cousin Mona and I would be wide-eyed from eavesdropping! Our aunts, having shared this one bathroom as children, had no issue with individual privacy; just gender separation seemed important. One could be on the toilet, one in the bathtub, one shaving her legs from the sink, and another putting on makeup. They made gross jokes about men not cutting their toenails and leaving wet towels on the bathroom floor. Once I remember Aunt Teddy saying that having a baby was like "passing a watermelon," and they all laughed madly. Her words were with me when I was about to give birth to my son.

Aunt Freida, the only sibling with the Fischer olive complexion, was especially wild and could have been a standup comic for sure. She used to leave her spearmint chewing gum on the back of the john to save for the next day. She never knew that I used to borrow it and put it back in the morning. To this day spearmint is my favorite-flavored chewing gum. Freda was married three times, twice to the same man.

Millie, the oldest, had the burden of looking after her younger brothers and sisters and always seemed older than she was in years. I remember when she was 40 years old she became engaged to an Errol Flynn look-alike called Horace. Cousin Mona and I hid behind the reading chair and watched them have a kissing session; we were knocked out by the sight. Aunt Millie had huge, luminous eyes. We all thought she looked like the movie star Loretta Young.

Aunt Marcella was a great beauty. She was a vocalist sometimes with local bands. She had natural platinum hair. Aunt Millie tells the story that one day she was walking past the Neil House Hotel on High Street in Columbus when walking toward her was "the most beautiful woman she had ever seen." It turned out it was her sister, Marcella.

Uncle Dick was the child who never left his mother. He fought in WWII and returned home an alcoholic. He would disappear for weeks and Mom would think he was dead, and then he would return completely out of his mind. I was visiting one summer when he came home and left his car running without the brakes locked and it went rolling down the hill, amazingly not harming anyone or anything—if you could see the landscape you would know it was a miracle!

He was very tall, lean, and quiet and spent hours listening over and over to a recording of "You're a Slow Poke." I can still sing the lyrics. "I wait and worry but you never seem to hurry. You're a slow poke. Time means nothing to you, I wait and then, late again. One o'clock, two o'clock, quarter to three," and so on.

My cousin Mona and I loved to watch him roll his cigarettes. Uncle Dick had lost part of his middle finger in WWII, but this did not interfere with his capacity for holding the white cigarette papers in the rest of his long, tapered fingers and tapping across the tobacco ending with a long, lazy lick to seal the roll. He would strike a large match to light up and raise his chin high, taking deep puffs and holding the cigarette only between his lips. The smell of the burning match and tobacco made it seem like a ritual. Uncle Dick appeared to enter a trance-like state, and we were awe-struck;

enough that we stole some of his stash and hid it in a Secrets Throat Lozenges tin.

We sneaked off to our hiding place by the pond called "the ship," actually a very large rock, and lighted up, imitating Uncle Dick's chin-high pose—and fell into spasms of coughing. The smoking myth, for me anyway, was over; sadly for Mona the love of smoking consumed her life.

Uncle Carl was the son who I am told most resembled my grandfather Theodore. He was very handsome, with beautiful dark hair combed back. He had a sunny disposition, and we two had a special bond. He always seemed to find me amusing, and we had great fun together; even with our age difference we understood each other like equals.

He moored a wonderful speedboat at the levee in downtown Pomeroy. We would tear around the Ohio River like jet fighters. His daughter, my cousin Birdie, and I would straddle the tip of the boat, holding onto a rope, and when it reached what seemed like warp speed the boat's nose would rise up; it was like riding in the rodeo. We loved it! It must have been very dangerous, but it never entered our minds to be afraid on the river. We would ride to Long Bottom Island and have a picnic, get sunburned, and laugh like loons.

Uncle Carl's voice was deep with a velvety, gentle tone—it was like hearing music when he spoke. To this day I consider him one of the best people I have known in my life. He was killed in an automobile accident in Kentucky by a careless driver who had passed on a curve, hitting him head on. Uncle Carl's death was my first experience with inconsolable grief. I thought we all would die from it. His widow, Aunt Julia, would never say that Carl was dead or killed; only that Carl "was hurt." She lost so much weight I thought only her shadow would last. Although today I am the last one standing, I still feel the loss of Uncle Carl from our family and am haunted by how it mirrored his own father's death at an early age.

The back porch of Mom's house stood firm against a steep drop down the hill that ended at the front gate of my great grandparents' house where my grandfather Theodore had been raised. My Bavarian great-grandmother, Ma, never learned English, rarely spoke, and spent most days sitting on the front porch swing with her little feet dangling high above the floor. She was always dressed in black with a little Amish hat on her head, puffing away on a corncob pipe. Her face was very weathered with deep folds and wrinkles. Contrasting with her dark swarthy complexion were her very light blue eyes, which had so much depth that you felt the secrets of the universe. She never moved from her own property, but she would observe our family on the hill above her as entertainment.

In her side yard was a wishing well, the water sweet and cool. Peering down into the bottomless darkness, I always felt I had risked my future for the pleasure. If Van Gogh had seen Ma he could have portrayed her as one of the potato eaters in his famous painting. He also would have painted her magnificent sugar pear tree with its twisted limbs and the petite golden pears that tasted of honey.

Inside, her home was furnished with heavy Victorian furniture, red velvet sofas, all very regal and formal looking, and quite a contrast to her. One of my two tangible Pomeroy treasures is a hand-painted serving platter with a Bavarian hunting scene that belonged to Ma. The other is a hand-painted pitcher from Bavaria that belonged to my great-great-grandfather. I refer to it as the Pomeroy pitcher.

My grandmother Mom kept her chickens at the bottom of the hill and would make the steep descent down the moss-covered stones to the chicken coop. When they heard those particular footsteps, the chickens, sensing they were on death row, would begin a chorus of loud clucking. She took a chicken once a week for Sunday dinner, the only meat day. In her own version of mercy killing, she wrung the chicken's neck in a second and then hung it on the clothesline for its feathers to be plucked.

One Easter I was given a purple chick, my favorite color, and Mom said she would keep it for me. Months later after a Sunday dinner, I learned I had just eaten my baby chick. I have felt closer to vegetables ever since.

The "P" Factor

It was a wonderful party in a beautiful club. I loved watching my Aunts dance with their husbands looking so elegant in their long dresses. Hair upswept seemed to be the "do" for the dance. Aunt Marcella was particularly striking with her premature platinum hair framing a luscious beauty of a face. She wore a violet gown, and she glowed in the candlelight. Her laugh was so melodious that it punctuated the rhythm of the music.

Sometimes she would lean back in a twirl, looking so joyful I thought that dancing must be the most important of human activities. I was so young, barely seeing over the round cabaret table, and felt privileged to observe what grownups do when they are not working. Everything, everyone changed when the big band would strike up "In the Mood" and the joyful rush to the dance floor.

My older cousin Ruth and her husband Dick were such expert dancers that the crowd would stop and watch them move with such skill and coordination it was breathtaking. It didn't hurt that Ruth was very beautiful with her raven hair and Dick a physical match. The Dorsey Brothers asked them to tour with the band, but they turned down the opportunity. My Aunt Teddy, the golden blond in the family, was her own brand of femme fatale, and

Tommy Dorsey was showing so much interest in her that her husband, Uncle Tewks, took a bite out of his cocktail glass. Oh it was delightful energy and I, the little sponge, took it all in.

I remember after a long period of dancing and almost manic sociability the band stopped playing. It was called a "BREAK," my aunts said, so people could get a drink and go to the bathroom. And so my aunts, Marcella, Teddy, Freida, and Millie, gathered me up to join them in the ladies room, an expression that was new to me. The room was very pretty with gold-framed mirrors and vanities and upholstered chairs and drapes that matched. In the adjoining room I heard flushing and realized it was a bathroom!

My aunts stopped at the mirrors and in unison opened their pretty evening bags to find their golden compacts to powder their noses, lipstick to be newly applied, and a comb to run quickly through their hair before they entered the bathroom stalls to "take a pee," as they would say. I had never had a chance to hear all my aunts go the bathroom at the same time. I listened to their individual what I called pee power. Some came very forcefully, some fitfully, some lasting what seemed a very long time. Wow, I thought, to be a real woman you really need to learn how to pee! As they waited outside the stall for me and my pitiful contribution, all I could think was that I had a lot of work to do on my pee power if I was to ever measure up to these extraordinary women.

I shyly came out of the stall and they all said how important it was to wash and dry my hands. They fussed over me a little, and I began to understand why the ladies room was so special. They laughed and talked like they were home together in Pomeroy. And to think men could never come in the door. Amazing! A very nice-looking elderly lady sat by the door with lotion, perfume, and real towels; her job was to assist us in this sacred place, and you were supposed to leave a tip on the table to thank her. I thought I always want to be in the ladies room with my aunts. I felt like I had been welcomed into an exclusive club.

As a mature woman, I can tell you the ladies room has more competition than the Miss America contest, and it involves way more than the P factor. Understanding the stall protocol, you wait in line for your turn and you don't take too long, and the women who know they are beautiful seem to take over the mirrors with their elbows out and are oblivious to you, an ordinary girl who would like to reach for a towel and maybe do a little retouch herself. But the competition is too great, so you just throw your towel into the trash, take a deep breath, and say, "Oh well, beauty is in the eye of the beholder and I bet she really has stinky breath." And you exit the ladies room with your own brand of dignity. Other times you have meaningful conversations that contribute to the girl bonding we crave since our mother's knee.

Women will talk about things in a loud voice in the ladies room that their shrink will never hear. Many times, the men's room is adjacent to the ladies and I wonder if they can hear what the girls say. I remember a woman who looked like she enjoyed all the material luxuries of life say in a loud voice, "I hope my next husband is RICH!" If he heard her, did he immediately think I should buy her a new trinket, or if he had any sense did he leave her with the check?

The code of entre nous in the ladies room has been passed from one generation of women to the next for a reason; it is a place for her to purge her body and soul. The P Factor is just an excuse to leave the hectic crowd for a protected place where her gender rules. It may be the only room of her own she shall ever know.

Whenever I enter an especially glamorous ladies room anywhere in the world, I pause a moment to remember my wonderful aunts and my initiation into this feminine culture where the sign on the door says it all.

Dream Kitchen

As a three-year-old, I remember the scale of life then. I, just tall enough to embrace my mother's knees, would stretch my little neck, straining to see what mysteries were being performed in this room. It had high counters and a sink with water where I would stand on a chair and help my mother wash the dishes and would make soap bubbles float into the air like wishes. Most awesome in this amazing room was a great wide door that, when opened, would blow hot air into your face. I felt fear and attraction every time Mamma would feed this hot-mouthed monster. Soon the house would smell so wonderful that my instinct to want it in my mouth was overwhelming. "When, Mamma? When, Mamma?" I would ask over and over, and she would reply, "Soon, soon, Carole."

Usually I would amuse myself by removing all the pots and pans from below the counter-top, and as I stepped inside Mamma would, ask, "Carole, where are you going?" I would reply, "New York City!" How could I know to say that?

Well, this particular day I decided I would not travel but instead I would help my mother with her kitchen duties without her permission. I remember straining my legs and my right arm to reach the counter and, to my horror, knocking the knife she was using to cut apples for a pie onto her foot, and blood began running to the floor. Thankfully, after that incident my mother would place projects on the kitchen table where I could sit on my knees and sprinkle sugar and cinnamon onto the leftover pie dough for snickerdoodles! The smell of the spice with the butter and sugar that filled the house is still one of my favorite aroma memories.

My passion for being in the kitchen began in these early years, and having a kitchen of my very own began to fill my dreams every night. These dreams were so vivid and fulfilling; nothing in my adult life has replaced the exciting virtual pleasure of imagining myself in my very own kitchen making delicious things in my own oven. My mother always wore aprons that she or her mother had made and embroidered, and so I, of course, wore very beautiful aprons too.

That Christmas, my last as an only child it turned out, I came down to a tree that had been decorated while I slept. There in all its majesty was my very own little kitchen, with a real electric Easy Bake Oven! My little kitchen also had a sink with running water for washing my dishes and baking pans plus storage cupboards. Now Mamma and I could bake side by side. And we did!

I made darling little cakes and pies, and she and I would have them with tea on my little plates and cups. The combination of having such a dream come completely true in every detail plus the deep pleasure of tea parties with my mother have made me believe in the power of our dreams.

How to Ruin Your Own Birthday Party

My mother planned my first birthday party when I was four. I don't recall who the guests were, but I remember vividly how the party played out.

From the day I left the womb I seemed not to like classic baby food that someone my age was supposed to eat. Of course with hindsight I realize I was allergic to milk, but in 1938 who would have even thought of such a thing in this dairy-dominant world we occupy in the West? Because milk made me sick it also made me very hard to live with on a day-to-day basis. My mother said I seemed to want orange juice and olives! So it figures that my idea of what tastes good might deviate from the norm.

"Carole honey, what do you want Mamma to make for your birthday party?"

"Mamma, I want my favorites—Waldorf salad and Ritz crackers."

"Okay baby, you can have anything you want," and of course she meant it. I don't think she gave the menu another thought. She sliced the apples, added celery, grapes, walnuts, and best of all, little marshmallows and dressed it with Miracle Whip like she always did. Oh yes, I also asked for iced tea. Sounded great!

I remember the long table with a paper cloth, and all the kids brought presents that really puzzled me. Why would they give away their stuff—I wouldn't! Obviously I hadn't been to a birthday party myself. "Okay kids, come to the table; it's time to eat," my mother called in her sweet voice.

All the kids sat down and she lay down a large bowl of Waldorf salad, the plate of Ritz crackers, and a pitcher of iced tea. Everyone got quiet. Then one of the kids said, "What's that?" Pointing to the food!

"Why this is what Carole wanted for her birthday—it is her favorite!!" Mother answered happily.

"Uck, where is the birthday cake, ice cream? Where is the Coca Cola?" All the kids chimed in, making a loud, threatening chant. My mother put her hand over her mouth and looked frightened.

One by one the guests grabbed the birthday presents they had brought me and bolted out the door. My mother was devastated; she had worked so hard to please me. I never trusted kids in a generic sense ever again, and I never wanted to have another birthday party! Thereafter I preferred quiet dinners with grownups.

Mamma never attempted another party in my name, and I was glad!

Hair Tricks!

Every child accepts its mother's way of doing everything. It is how you learn. I confess, however, to the buds of suspicion as my life extended into my mother's world. As a growing child I had accepted with some patience that I had to wear the same outfit every day—an exact copy of Alice in Wonderland or Judy Garland in the blue dress with a white organdy pinafore from *The Wizard of Oz*. But the other obsession my mother had, my hair, was another matter. She was determined that I should have long, tubular curls like Shirley Temple. What I later referred to as "Mamma's Hair Tricks" included extreme efforts to accomplish the perfect hairdo for her daughter.

Because my hair is plentiful but far from obedient it has been known to unfurl a curl and toss a bobby pin across a table. I understood its defiance and admired it, really. Because of the short time my hair would hold this tableau of curls made possible by thick slimy wave set, Mamma decided I needed one of the new hair-curling tricks at the local beauty parlor.

"Vie, I can't get this child's hair to do anything. It is so contrary—could you perm it?"

Vie answered, "Well she's pretty young to have her hair permed."

"Oh, don't worry, Vie, we can put her on some phone books and shoeboxes, don't you think?"

"Well, maybe," Vie said with worry in her voice that even I can hear.

Soon I was lifted up onto a pile of various books so the electrical cords and hair clamps could reach my frightened hair. In today's world I would say the scene resembled an electric chair used for executions. I was terrified, but I didn't cry. Mother kept saying, "Carole, your hair is going to be naturally curly after this – wait and see!"

Poor Mamma. Her high hopes for my hair soon went up in flames; my hair actually caught fire! Vie began screaming, "Edith, Carole's hair is on fire! Pull the plug!" Vie was frantically snatching the individual electrical cords off my hair, saying with each disconnect, "Oh, my God! Oh my God!" The shop reeked of the smell of burned hair!

Mother cried and cried—I don't think she cried for me but for my lost hair. Her hair dreams had been so dashed, and now my hair had to be cut really short. So short, in fact, that I had some bald spots in the back.

This experience is emblematic of other hair trick stories I will not tell here, but I can say that when I got out on my own, no one touched my hair until I was in my thirties. To this day I avoid hair salons and rely mostly on my own hair tricks—a talent I most probably inherited from a woman called Edith Mae who was my mother.

Sleeping in My Bed!

When I was four years old and without any warning, I can remember my mother came home with a baby boy, my brother Scotty. I had gone to visit my Grandma and Grandpa Stewart and returned home to find that I had been removed from my bedroom and this intruder had taken my bed. I swear I had no idea she was having a baby! As well as I can recall my childhood, how can it be that I have no recollection of my mother including me in the news that now I would no longer be an only child! Well, I can tell you with absolute authenticity, I did not like this boy coming into my home. Nothing could soften my attitude about him; I wanted him gone!

I remember watching him like he was prey. I stalked him and finally came up with a plan to be rid of him. I went into my father's tie rack and chose a tie I liked and slipped into my former bedroom where my little brother lay sleeping in my bed. I could barely reach the wooden crib rungs where I threaded the tie under his chin and was just about to begin pulling when my mother came into the room. You can imagine her horror at learning she had a potential four-year-old murderer in the house!

As Mamma would say many times in her life, if Scotty had been like me, she could not have survived. He was so sweet, docile, quiet—nothing like his renegade sister. The good nature of my brother also affirmed her belief that God does not give a person more than she can handle. With me this belief had been very challenged.

Some of the years with Scotty are a blur, but I do know I never again tried to kill him! Over time he became my little brother whom I adored and protected. And I have the physical scars to prove it. One afternoon I overheard a neighbor girl beating up on Scotty. Being in my Wonder Woman phase, I flew in and found her hitting him with a belt! I took on Donna Jane myself. She bit me so hard on my right wrist that I will go into my death fires with the dental imprint of her two front teeth! She was a mean little thing and used to chide my brother with the chant, "Scotty Stewart has a wart, right between his legs!"

Scotty had cornstalk blond hair and light blue eyes except when he would sneak into the Kanawha River for a swim and return with eyes that were bloody red and hair made dark from the oily water.

"Scotty have you been in the river?"

"No Mamma, I haven't been in the river," all the while reeking from the smell of chemicals. She would believe him! I could never have gotten by with such a fib.

My brother was a mechanical genius; he collected bits and pieces that were tossed away and could make a bicycle! He also had a great green thumb and grew the best vegetables. We traded Christmas presents because he wanted to play with my dolls and I wanted his toy guns. I was the wild tomboy and he was the sweet child.

Scotty would grow up to be a regular Jimmy Dean, riding motorcycles, racing cars in Spain, and later helping to build the first airstrip in Camrarh Bay in Vietnam. His life-long career in the Air Force would keep him and his family out of the country most of the time. His favorite bar in Spain was the same one as the writer Ernest Hemingway's. His horizons expanded well beyond our West Virginia days and fed his southern knack of telling wonderful stories.

Scotty remained a gentle, sweet, and kind person. I believe he got his goodness from our mother. Truth is, I am more like my restless dad. My mother certainly deserved such a wonderful son, and I was blessed to call him brother. I am grateful both Mamma and Poppa didn't live to know that Agent Orange and the resulting cancer killed him at far too young an age.

Today, I would kill to give my bed to my brother.

Cat Tails

The house in Upper Belle was near the river's edge where incredible cattails grew, giving the illusion of solid land to walk upon. My dad sat me down and warned of this deception, telling me, "Never go into the cattails because you could drown!" Newly bruised from recent exploits, I decided I should listen to him for a change. Added to the cattails' danger was a house being built near the river's edge. Daddy also warned me to "stay away" from the construction site because it, too, was very hazardous.

So much to resist with Poppa going off to work leaving time and opportunity for a little adventure. Too much temptation for a curious girl, indeed, and the call of the cattails got the best of me!

I am told that I was a very agile child with long legs, long pigtails, and most interesting, a tiny mole just over the tip of my lip that my mother considered a "natural beauty mark."

The construction site seemed to me a stage calling for a performance, and the cattails would be my audience. I began my untrained version of a ballet solo, leaping like a winged creature from one foundation block to another with a great ode to joy! Suddenly, like a bird being shot in mid-flight, I stumbled and fell onto a long construction nail sticking out of the foundation. It stabbed me through my upper lip, removing forever my natural beauty mark mole!

Blood was gushing, and my face was swelling as I ran home calling for my mother. She screamed, "Oh Daddy," when she saw me and nearly fainted. Of course, Daddy had to come home from DuPont. I remember having to get a tetanus shot that scared me to death. However, the indelible memory of that night is that my dad didn't spank me or raise his voice as he would usually. Instead, he spoke calmly and reasoned with me about the choices I make. It was my first adult conversation as a child, and I actually understood what he was trying to teach me.

We both learned something that night, and it brought to an end the use of threats and spankings to control my behavior. This truce lasted for a very long time before he was forced for the final time to lay a hand on me for punishment.

Years later in my serious, femme fatale days, I would take a black eyebrow pencil and mark a fake mole just over the tip of my right lip, and it always felt just right, like it belonged there.

A natural beauty mark!

Carte Blanche

My parents moved from Ohio to Belle, West Virginia, when my father took a position with DuPont shortly after I was born. Our first home was in Upper Belle, where the amenities of a town existed, blocks of homes, churches, a small residential hotel where old men sat out front with their canes, a pharmacy, a hair salon, an ice cream parlor, and a train station.

In Upper Belle my dad could walk to his favorite grocery store called Secrist's Market, owned by Bill of the same name. I loved going to the market with my dad and seeing all the food. Daddy was very particular about his meat and would tell the butcher how to carve his favorite T-bone steaks. He always told me, "Honey, you should always support your local businessman."

Being "knee high to a grasshopper," as my dad would say, I could lean on his lower leg and watch hopefully for the extraordinary appearance of a very tall, broad woman known as Dora. She would appear carrying a huge deep velvet purse, from which she extracted a large silver serving spoon. Ignoring everyone, she would stride to the freezer, scrape ice from its sides, and eat it! She had a glazed look in her eyes like an animal that was consuming its prey.

Daddy and Bill took no notice of her, but I would stare, mouth wide open! Dora was always dressed beautifully in clothes that floated around her large frame, giving the impression she had wings. She also wore a stylish hat and perfume whose heavy scent lingered in the store long after she had swept out the door. I never saw Dora speak to anyone or buy anything at Secrist's Market.

I did pick up some important information shopping with my dad that became useful later—or so I thought at the time. When leaving with our groceries, Daddy would always say, "Put it on my bill, Bill!" I was very impressed—so this is how you get stuff!

That fall I began first grade and was horrified to learn such places as schools existed. I had no interest in being held hostage in a room with a bunch of kids I didn't know. I was pleased to learn the word recess meant I could go outside and play and be free for a bit. Eventually I made friends with some of my classmates and one beautiful spring day decided it would be great to leave the playground during recess and take a rather long walk to Secrist's Market. I invited my new chums along and bought them all ice cream bars and told the cashier, using my father's voice, "Put it on my bill, Bill!"

Of course, we did not make it back to school in time and caused a major scandal, of which I was the star! I think my dad was so amazed at my initiative that he was rendered helpless. For a while I was apparently too well known in the community. A policy of containment was established between Bill and Daddy whereby only Daddy could speak the magic phrase in the future. My mother, on the other hand, who would not step foot in a grocery store herself, was frightened by my assertiveness and could only utter her usual, "Child are you trying to kill me?" Maybe I am the reason we moved to Lower Belle, where no grocery stores existed?

Willow Switches

I was very contrite after any of my exploits that turned out badly. I would promise Mamma and myself that I would never, ever, again be bad. Oh, but being good was terribly hard—I had this energy that would overtake me and off I would go into unexplored waters yet again, just asking to drown!

I just could not adjust to the rigors and confinement of going to school. Many a day Momma would come out to shake a dust mop and find her wild daughter sitting on the back steps, having run away yet again. She would be very upset with me and walk me back to school. The walk to school was rather daunting for a five-year-old, and I was always worried I would take a wrong turn and not find my way home. The teacher would act nice to my mother but look at me with red, beady eyes after she left.

And so the tradition of the willow tree switches began. I had a pet willow tree I loved and would hide under when I didn't want anyone to know where I was. When the school would contact my mother to inform her that I was again missing, I could hear her crying and it would make me so sad that I would break off some willow branches and take them to her as an offering of contrition.

"Mamma, if I am ever bad again, you can whip me with these willow switches," I would say, and without exception I never made it through the day without feeling the sting of the switches on my backside. Sometimes my remorse wouldn't last long enough to accept the actual punishment, and when her hand was raised to whip me with one of the switches, I would start running around and around our dining table to make her dizzy and then suddenly reverse directions and run out the door to hide outside.

And so the willow switch circle of contrition did not always end in my redemption but in more damnation. The pledge to be forever good remained an unsolved contest between my mother and me for many years. Although the memory of my dear mother's face when she was forced to punish me stings, the weeping willow tree remains my favorite, with its graceful tendrils forming a beautiful skirt of greenery into which a person can retreat and dream.

Not a Lark!

My second-grade teacher, Miss Lark, seemed perpetually frozen in a rage with her neck bones always protruding, probably because the word "kill" was locked inside her gritted teeth. Just say the word "kill" and you will see for yourself how it changes your face.

She had the practice of calling randomly on a student to go out into the school hallway and to report back to her and the class what time it was from the hall clock. I lived in mortal fear of the day when my name, Carole Elaine Stewart, would be the deadly peal from her icy lips. My dear mother spent many hours in the evening teaching me how to tell time to prepare me for that inevitable unfortunate day. When another student's name was called I felt a brief state of relief. However, the feeling of being on death row soon returned as each new hour brought a new threat.

It was afternoon when the dreaded day came. Miss Lark intoned my name like the tolling of the bells. The smallest child in her class, I shrunk smaller still and under her cold, stern stare began the macabre march into the hallway where I pressed my back against the tile wall and slid down to the floor under the clock and began weeping violently.

Because I did not return to the class, Miss Lark sought me out in the hallway and dragged me back into the classroom screaming. She forced my fingertips, pulling them backwards so that my palm was rigid. Holding me in a hammerlock with her bony elbow she reached for her brass-edged ruler and began beating the inside of my palm while my classmates watched with horror.

I remember nothing else about that school year, just that day. Miss Lark is frozen in my childhood, never to thaw, and the fire and fear remain imprinted in my left hand. Don't ask me what time it is. I shall never be able to say.

Teaching Little Fingers

That was the title of my first piano lesson exercise book by John Thompson: *Teaching Little Fingers How to Play*. Practicing the piano meant playing endless scales, repetitions, Mamma beside me cheering me on. "Carnival of Animals," by Saint Saens had a melody I really liked and made the struggle of piano competency more worth the monotony. My restless, tomboy energy was hard to channel into our maple spinet, but my mother was obsessed with the idea that I should master this refinement and hopefully someday become a more respectable-acting young lady.

Of course looking down from the heights of my own maturity, I realize now that Mamma wanted me to have what she had been denied with the death of her father and the poverty that engulfed the family striking down such luxuries as piano lessons. "Listen to the metronome, dear; it will be your drum beat and help you keep your rhythm." A lost cause, alas; to this day no metronome can tell me what my pace of movement should be! I just know that faster always seemed just right.

In the second grade I had to give up my lunch hour once a week to go across the street from the school to take piano lessons from a woman who looked exactly like Carmen Miranda! Her hair was wrapped high with bold colors that I had never seen on another living person. She had long, long fingers, accentuated with three-inch fingernails polished blood red! She liked music in the minor key and would be considered very postmodern in today's world. Finding no melody upon which to cling, I would make one mistake after another. Munching on a red delicious apple, she would regularly reach over with her witch's nails and dig a slight scratch into my hands and arms that drew blood.

Thank God Mamma took me away from this sadist, and I began taking lessons from a wonderful, handsome man who was probably my mother's age. We would take the bus to Charleston, have lunch, and go on to Mr. Fischer's studio. He was my first real crush outside the movies. He was tall with black hair combed back neatly, and he had wonderful features. I blossomed under his tutelage and moved onto concertos. His studio was in a record store, and he would have me listen to the music before I ever began learning it. These outings were special for both my mother and me, and I think that there was a special spark between my mother and my teacher. It was nice to see her appearing in a different role than the one she played at home. Years later, Mr. Fischer left teaching to become a concert pianist and we never saw him again. I believe it was one of the best times for mother—a candle burning briefly that gave her some independence and freedom.

Another great thing about Mr. Fischer was that he did not have piano recitals. However, under my new teacher this was not the case. My first piano recital was a huge occasion for my mother. I had my first evening gown when I was seven years old. It was yellow, ruffled, off the shoulders, and with ruffles down to the floor—a miniature Scarlet O'Hara was I. "Fur Elise" was the piece I was to play, and Mamma and I would go about the house la, la, la, la la ing the tune. I loved how music brought us together. But looking forward to the actual recital was torture for me—I started getting sick thinking about it in December and suffered until that fateful day in May when we performers were all lined up backstage waiting, in my opinion, for our executions! I cried quietly until the critical moment when I was shoved on stage—the transformation from dark to light, all the faces, the colors of the audience and most of all my beautiful mother sitting in the front row smiling, beaming with such pride. I smiled at her, reached for the corners of my gown, bowed, turned to the piano, and played perfectly. Applause, smiles, and it was over!

Later that summer while my parents were off shopping, my friends and I decided we should act out a "Sheena, Queen of the Jungle" story from a recent serial we had seen at the movies. As the only girl, I was to be Sheena; so I cut off my yellow evening gown to make it real short and tied the ruffles on to a long pole that I waved high over my head.

At that very moment my parents drove into our driveway and my memory goes blank.

What I do remember is that for the rest of my life I understood why Mamma would roll her eyes back and say about me, "You lik'da killed me."

Needles and Pins

I held my breath and closed my eyes. What would hurt me first, the lighted cigarette or the needle headed directly into my outer upper arm? The local doctor with his yellow-stained fingers would rub the spot where I should have a tetanus shot. How he managed to keep his cigarette in the same hand that held the hypodermic needle is a test of his amazing dexterity, but to the recipient of what I considered a two-pronged horror, it was very frightening.

I did not enter this contest freely. The required tetanus shot for attending summer camp was an annual event viewed from both sides of the needle with resistance. As soon as I realized what I was in for, I would begin running around the examination table screaming, "No! No!" Mother would follow, imploring me to stop, insisting that it wasn't going to hurt (LIE!) and it would soon be over. The doctor and his nurse would run in opposite directions and I would be captured and held down screaming like a wild animal.

It is unfortunate that my association with this trauma precluded any hope of my being fond of the doctor's son. He was in my first-grade class and seemed especially devoted to me. He gave me my first grown-up size box of chocolates in a beautiful red heart-shaped box for Valentine's Day. Maybe he is responsible for my liking this holiday above all others for the rest of my life. Maybe that would make him happy to know I remember him in this way. I do remember his name, but he shall remain anonymous here. I kept the physician's son psychologically on needles and pins while his father kept me physically in the same condition. Oh irony, how cruel your sense of symmetry!

My dear mother also dreaded taking me to the dentist, where I would need to be strapped down. I fought and screamed and one day I bit the dentist, who retaliated with a very hard slap to my face. I needed to have a tooth pulled, and I remember the dentist sweating over me and his knees pressed against my body to keep me pinned down. When I heard the cracking sound in my head as the tooth gave way, I fainted.

The wild beast inside of me kept the fear of needles and pins alive well into my adulthood. As a young, independent woman I managed to stay away from such moments until I had to have a blood test to get married. It was a big decision for me! And the birth of my son was the next challenge with this fear.

Arriving at the hospital after my water had broken on a very hot Washington, D.C., August night, I was whisked away in a wheelchair while my husband parked the car. It was 1963, and men did not participate in the birthing of babies. A frail little man pushed me down the narrow hospital corridor, suddenly taking a sharp right turn and letting go of the wheelchair, sending me flying down a ramp toward two heavy doors. They opened at the last second and I arrived screaming into the actual delivery rooms. Women all around in various stages of screaming pain frightened me, so I began crying, saying I wanted my mother!

A skinny, mean nurse pinned my legs apart with her elbows and began shaving my pubic hair. I was shivering so violently I could have been a cricket vibrating my legs to call out an SOS. This little witch in a white uniform rolled me into a prison-like room with cracked walls and chained my wrist to a metal bed that had ether in what looked like a tea strainer. All I could see was an institutional clock with big black numbers and hands. Not one person said a kind word to me, and I was left alone feeling so cold I thought I would freeze to death.

It turned out that my doctor was on vacation and I fell between the cracks of anyone paying attention to me. After Rob was born, I felt very unwell, and the hospital staff seemed to imply I was just a weak sister. On the fifth night, an orderly took me down the hall and placed me into a sitz bath that was practically floor level and was supposed to be warm but was cold instead. Hours later, after calling for help to deaf ears, I literally crawled back to my room.

The next day a wonderful nurse—a real one it turns out, the first I had seen since I checked into the house of horrors—took my temperature and said, "You poor baby, you have a high fever and you are fighting a serious infection." Her compassion was like a drink of holy water; it restored my hope that I would actually live to take care of my son. It turned out most of the nurses had been on vacation. Plus, the attending doctor hadn't given me a thought after the actual birth, which explains why I had not received qualified treatment.

Move the calendar way up and I am in the labor room with my daughter-in-law, my son by her side helping her with breathing exercises to mediate the pain. The room is beautifully furnished to look like a lovely home. She has pictures of their Dalmatian dog, Sammie, to focus on when the pain is too sharp. Only when the baby is cresting would she be moved a few feet into a room for the actual birth. She had windows to look out over the city. I can't help but think of the differences time has brought and be grateful.

When other mothers would describe giving birth as the most wonderful experience of their lives, I would always remain silent. Yes, having my son Rob was, and is, the greatest experience of my life except for the actual experience of giving birth. The other gift was letting go of my fear of needles and pins!

The Day the Sky Fell

It is a perfect summer morning—Mamma is baking her wonderful bread—the Pomeroy bread. My little brother Scotty and I wait like vultures for the first feeding—warm bread and fresh butter. After the bread feast, I go to my room and open my junk drawer and pull out my red ribbon with the hairpin always attached to begin my day as the youngest retail person in Lower Belle.

The DuPont factory that looms over our two-story brick house is belching its daily sulfur-smelling air. The nearly invisible coal dust is turning my lungs into a polka-dotted pattern that keeps me frail, but that is another story. Today I head to the factory gate beside the Kanawha River and watch the ferry bring workers across from Marmet. I loved saying Marmet—even at age six I knew it sounded elegant and should be a faraway place. That day the river had changed its chemical coat to a deep ruby red and the ferry carved a curvaceous pattern in the river as it moored on the Belle side.

Barefoot, but with my red ribbon in my slightly combed hair, I was ready to greet the workers: "Newspapers, 10 cents!" Several bought papers and smiled at me, and occasionally I would get a tip. My favorite worker lived on my side of the river and always looked so handsome in his freshly ironed blue shirts. He carried his lunchbox, and I bet he had special food too. Somebody really cared for him.

Later my favorite worker walked by and his shirt was shredded, his lunchbox was missing, and blood was dripping from his face; I began screaming. At that moment a plane flew over and the sky began to fall! The ground was covered with white papers—SCABS! All the papers had printed this one word, scabs! At the main entrance to the DuPont factory gunshots were fired and a man was killed.

I ran into the house crying and warning mother that something awful was happening outside. She and my brother, not used to seeing me hysterical, looked very worried. She tried to call Daddy and learned that a labor union was trying to forcibly organize the DuPont employees and they were trapped inside the factory. Actually Daddy spent the next two weeks a prisoner inside the factory; food and air mattresses had to be air-dropped in to sustain them throughout the ordeal.

And so the summer the sky fell I finally understood what Mamma meant when she would shake her head and say, "This life and the fireworks." It summed up the unexpected twists and turns of life. While Daddy was a prisoner inside the factory, Mamma, my little brother Scotty, and I were prisoners outside. Hemmed in between the river and the mountains, with no sidewalks, we could not get to Upper Belle on the other side of the factory to shop, and it would have been too dangerous to have walked past the factory anyway.

Mother had never gone grocery shopping. Daddy would bring the groceries home and she would then know what she was making for dinner. I don't remember how we managed, but we did, and just as suddenly everything was back to normal. Daddy returned home to us like a war hero, and I returned to the riverfront entrance to sell my papers. And Mother waited for Daddy to go grocery shopping.

Because of this experience I hated labor unions for years. It wasn't until my Aunt Millie, who worked for Columbus Bolt and Forging Company for 30 years assembling Oldsmobile parts, told stories about how the unions had protected workers like her that I understood the other side of the story.

Like the memory of orange and yellow fire flames dancing on my bedroom walls, the summer when the sky fell made a lasting impression on my soul.

Poppa Moose

For reasons unknown even to me, I just always called my dad "Poppa Moose." Actually, he looked a lot like the actor Robert Mitchum, except he was better looking.

Daddy spent most of his time away from us. He was either working or hunting with the guys or taking us to Pomeroy where he would leave us with my grandmother. He would go to Racine and stay with his mother until it was time to return to West Virginia. It all seemed perfectly normal. It was the '40s, after all, and everything domestic centered on the father's wants and needs. Mother was the perfect wife, doing everything "Daddy" liked. She catered to his every preference.

I remember my father's mother, my grandmother Stewart, and witnessed how far pleasing the man of the house could extend. Grandpa Stewart drilled for oil and was a very powerful figure physically. He didn't interact with us very much. All his wishes were manifested through his wife. Grandmother Stewart lived to please her husband, and that included keeping completely separate my grandfather's eating utensils. He had his own plates, glasses, cups, and flatware, and they were stored in a separate cupboard to be touched only by his wife. He only ate either angel food cake or devil's food chocolate cake desserts.

Being a true Scot, Daddy like his father enjoyed his drinks and would have loved the pub life of Britain; instead he spent his time in what we called beer joints. In Lower Belle where we lived, his favorite was the El Chico. It was a dark, salty-smelling place. Chico, the owner, was always at the bar, and Daddy sat at his favorite barstool with a cold Miller beer in his hand. Mother, who was against his drinking, would never go near the place, and certainly my younger brother could not go inside; hence, it was left to me to go to El Chico and bring my father home. I would run down the street and climb the short hill to the beer joint door that faced Route 60. I remember the neon sign that welcomed travelers to stop in for a drink and bar food. Everyone looked up when I came in—I would head directly to the bar, reach up, and pat my dad's back.

"Poppa Moose, Mamma wants you to come home for dinner. She has made your favorites: turnip salad, roast, and chocolate pie. You need to come home now and eat it while it's hot, okay Poppa?"

Daddy's bloodshot eyes would look proudly at me and he would smile. "Honey, sit up here and I will buy you a pickled egg!" He was really stalling for time to finish his beer.

"Not now, Poppa. We need to get home."

"Okay, honey. Well Chico, I guess I better get this little girl home." Chico would nod his head up and down and say nothing.

Then Daddy would tap a headache powder into his mouth throw his head back and down an entire bottle of beer without swallowing until the end. It was amazing. I bet he could have been in the circus swallowing swords! This always impressed me. I would realize many years later that Poppa Moose had a drinking addiction, but it never interfered with his important position at DuPont. He only drank when he was off duty. He would spend his leisure time with people who liked to drink, and that eliminated a lot of family time we could have had. His drinking made my mother sad, and she felt left out of his life. She could have joined him in this passion, but because of alcoholism in her own family I think she just could not bring herself to do so, even if it cost her my father's complete devotion.

My happiest times with Poppa Moose were when he would drive us to Pomeroy after the night shift and as we sped through the dark night we would all sing songs: "Blue Moon," "Star Dust," etc. He and Mamma would look at each other and smile while they shared a duet, and from the back seat I could feel their love for each other.

The River and the Red Ribbon

The sound of calliope music meant the river boats were coming through our locks on the Kanawha River! I would race to get the red ribbon for my hair, jump on my bicycle, and be in the crowd of other kids waving to the happy river travelers. As the boat passed through the locks we had close eye contact with the passengers. Some of the folks on board in an inebriated state were especially happy; I would dance a jig and they would throw money. "This is for the little girl with the red ribbon"—a five-dollar bill! That ribbon was like magic! I always got the most money so I would take my friends to the Camphite candy store for a treat, sharing my bounty to keep jealousy at bay.

At sunset I would return to the locks to watch the American flag being lowered by an old man who was employed by the River Authority. I wore my red ribbon for this ceremony, which was conducted in complete silence. I never knew the old man's name or he mine, but we repeated our pantomime with the same reverence each evening. I remember his large, weathered hands and their protruding veins. He would bow his head a bit to say, "Good evening little lady," with a smile; I would bow and say, "Good evening sir." The colors of the sunset would sink into the horizon, and the ritual of the river and the lowering of the flag would briefly erase the chemical reality of life in Belle, West Virginia. I know it sounds like a scene from a Shirley Temple movie. Well, it could have been!

Saturday Night and the Ladies

In our small neighborhood in Lower Belle most of the husbands worked for DuPont. That left Saturday night free for the wives when the men were on the night shift, and that is when my mother would set our neighbors' hair so they would look their best for church Sunday morning in Upper Belle.

Soon a huge box of bobby pins had been liberated into the hair of the women. They laughed and told stories about their husbands, and there was a liveliness and freedom that could not have happened on any other night of the week. Dinner was like a party at which we shared food and treats.

While our mothers were having their own little party, we kids would create our own special event. I remember hanging bark cloth drapes to create a theater in our garage and planning our talent show; we would bring chairs out into the driveway for our mothers to sit on and watch our show. A lot of the casting choices I made were based on getting my hands on my friends' dance costumes. I longed to take dance lessons, but my mother had committed me to piano and it was not negotiable. In love with the glamorous movie musicals, I longed to be Betty Grable.

I remember creating my own version of tap dancing and performing a rather demonic rendition to "I'm

Looking Over a Four-Leaf Clover." With verses that did not exist I extended my stage time in my friend Dian's green and white dance recital costume. I placed Donna Jane, the least-talented girl in the show, on a swing blowing bubbles throughout all the performances. Both she and her mother were pleased with her role.

Behind our garage the orange glow of the DuPont factory and its black smoke cast shadows over the moon, adding to our special effects. We ended the show with a sing-along, and everyone went home feeling happy.

Skin Deep

Mamma was thrilled that I was selected to be in a musical and would have a solo. After all she had been, by all accounts, the star in her senior class play! Although she never mentioned it, many people told me she was wonderful playing an eccentric old woman very realistically and had received a standing ovation. And so, living a little vicariously, she was very excited that I should be on stage and insisted on making my costume. It was a sweet little very short yellow dress with matching ribbons for my pigtails.

When rehearsals began I learned my role was that of a little black girl. We had no students of color at the time, so for me to play the part it required that most of my body be covered in black stage makeup. Mother was very upset because she figured my costume would be ruined with stains from the paint!

I was thrilled to be on stage with my grade-school crush, Gary Walker, who would sit between his future wife and me in the movies and hold both our hands. Gary was to be my grandfather, sitting in a rocking chair, and I was to sing and dance to a song whose lyrics included, "Sittin' in the sun, countin' my money, watching the clouds roll by... hearing those jingles upon the roof shingles like pennies, nickels and dimes, though it's known that all I own is not a large amount; clouds of gold that I behold are in my bank account … and to top it all when shadows fall, I look up into the heavens and I see there's a silver lining in each cloud just waiting for you and me!" I was barefoot on stage and improvised a dance. I had no speaking part.

The show was a hit, and I quite enjoyed being part of the cast and feeling special. The fun ended when I went home and my makeup needed to be removed. Mamma had me in the bathtub, weeping, "Oh child, I will never get this makeup off your skin," as she scrubbed my body for the third time with bathtub scouring powder! The following week my skin had a subtle tinge of grey decorated with red and pink abrasions! Not to mention the ring around the tub that looked liked it was planning to stay indefinitely.

It was a painful reentry into ordinary life and led me to the conclusion that in the future I would much prefer writing a play than being one of its stars! Applause was a fleeting reward. I broke this rule one time in college years later, but that tale I'll save for later. This memory for me, however, remains skin deep.

Bottle Envy

Every night at bedtime the DuPont factory would release its fiery coke ovens and a great, hot brilliant cascade of flaming coke would light the night sky. The bedroom window faced the ovens, the bright orange and yellow flames would flash dance through the room, and I expected to be incinerated nightly. For this reason I hated my bedroom. I also hated sharing the bedroom with my younger brother, Scotty. We had twin maple beds. I hated maple furniture. I hated my bed and its brown and orange bedspread.

And I hated facing a closet door that was always open with lots of clothes hanging on it. Many nights the hanging clothes on the door would viciously transform into what I believed with all my heart was a noose with a dead man dangling and the killer most likely hiding under my bed just waiting for me to foolishly drift off to sleep.

The one site I loved in my bedroom was my dressing table. It had an oval mirror attached that held the precisely arranged bottles of mostly real French perfume that Aunt Lee Lee had given me over the years. They were not new bottles, but they had a little perfume left inside so that I could pull out the glass stopper from the bottle top and dab my earlobes just like a movie star.

I particularly loved the Arpege bottle, black with gold letters. Aunt Lee Lee would often quote the slogan "Every woman needs Arpege!" I remember Dior's Intoxication, Caron's Bellogia, Joy, the most expensive perfume in the world at the time, and more working-class bottles like the lapis blue Evening in Paris I had bought for myself at Woolworth's. Emeraude was Aunt Millie's favorite, and my mother admired an English Penhaligons Carnation and of course Chanel No. 5 and No. 9. Aunt Lee Lee changed perfumes according to the season.

The bottles made up for all that was not agreeable in the chamber of horrors called my bedroom. I would spend hours arranging them just so. My mother thought I was obsessed and I can understand why—I never saw any perfume bottles in her room. I should say the room she shared with my father had only his things—keys, coins, shoe polish, sporting magazines—but nothing personal of my mother's. I know she used powder and lipstick, but where she kept her beauty supplies I know not. She had beautiful skin and really didn't need the cosmetics that many of her sisters used.

It was a beautiful spring afternoon. I had just come home from school and for some reason I went racing in to look at my collection of perfume bottles. What I found was a highly polished dressing table smelling of Pledge and one large Miracle Whip jar with a couple inches of a tea-colored liquid. I started screaming: "Mamma, Mamma, where are my perfume bottles?!"

She came in the room wiping her hands on her apron and said, "Oh, those bottles—I got tired of dusting them—I threw them away. Don't worry; I saved the perfume for you." She held up the Miracle Whip jar and seemed to be proud of how she had compromised to satisfy both our wishes.

"Oh Mamma, how could you?"

"Oh Carole, where do you get these ideas?" I cried so hard I thought my eyes would break.

Years later in my own home, Mamma threw away some valuable collectors' plates; I still miss them along with my perfume bottles. Truth is, she worked herself up to larger purges. I came home one day to find my dining room furniture gone; she had called the Salvation Army to come and take it away. "I knew you didn't like your furniture so I thought you would like to get rid of it," was her explanation. In her mind she was helping me. Months later I went to the basement to bring up my summer clothes and discovered she had given away my clothes! "Oh I thought you didn't need them," she explained.

I suppose it will seem strange to say that I never ever got mad at my mother. It is interesting to realize that I reached a crossroads about her at an early age and chose to find humor in her behavior and not pretend ever that she was like anyone else. These aberrations were just added to the folklore of Edie Mae.

Let's face it; I would be missing my reason for writing these memories were it not for my birthright as her daughter, Carole (named for Mamma's favorite actress, Carole Lombard, who later married mother's favorite actor Clark Gable); Elaine (the name of the girl my father was engaged to marry before meeting Mamma); Fisher (her maiden name); Stewart, Mamma's married name!

PS: I can recall how each perfume smelled to this day and have never bought myself a bottle of real perfume!

Summertime, and Living was a Gamble

My city cousin Mona from Columbus, Ohio, came to visit me in Lower Belle, West Virginia, where she saw how the DuPont plant dominated our town like a cathedral with a volcano as its steeple. Our chemically polluted, semi-rural environs were so different from her city existence that she may as well have been visiting a foreign country.

In the summer, we kids never wore shoes and ran fast on the unpaved streets to keep from burning our feet. Only our imaginations offered themes for playing and filling the hot summer days with excitement. The Kanawha River, the plant, and the railroad tracks by the mountainside confined our kingdom on three sides in a one-block area. This was our stage where we created intrigue and adventure.

Mamma never batted an eye when suddenly the front door would swing open and a rock would be thrown into the hall with a love note wrapped around it saying it was from Zorro! It was the alias of my next-door neighbor BD, who had a crush on me and showed his devotion by flinging rocks into my home.

The brothers, Ping and BD, were my daily playmates, and we managed to make every summer day a movie script in which we all starred. On this day we decided to show Mona the Kanawha River locks. Trees grew thick on the river bank, and because of the locks the lower bank was covered with a cement wall; wild vines curled through the trees like snakes. We would grab a vine and swing out over the river and back to the hilltop. It was dangerous, and we loved swinging out into fate's arms, not knowing if we would return safely to shore. It was an addicting exhilaration!

On this particular hot afternoon, Mona, Ping, BD, and I sat watching the locks when suddenly Ping decided he was Tarzan, King of the Jungle, grabbing me with one arm and a wild grapevine with the other and screaming "Me Tarzan—you Jane"! I remember feeling like I was in slow motion as we dangled over the river and finally snapping back toward the shore, past the stone walls, and then BANG! Blackness. I remember seeing stars that I will later in life recognize in a Van Gogh painting and struggling to breathe. I can hear my cousin crying and yelling, "You killed my Cuzzie, you killed my Cuzzie," as she pummeled Ping!

Poor Ping, who was a bit overweight, had landed dead on top of me when the vine snapped and I was knocked unconscious. Slowly I came back to life and we four sat for a long time on the hill without talking—each realizing we had escaped a close call. That summer the Tarzan and Jane show ended.

Walking home we spotted a persimmon tree, and although we didn't know what kind of fruit it was, we could not resist its beauty. We each picked one and began to eat with gusto. Within seconds the unripe persimmon had its revenge—our mouths puckered and we were sure we had been poisoned! We all four began spitting profusely! It took quite a while to feel normal again, if that was ever possible. I felt we had been banished from the Garden of Eden, and I am frightened of persimmons to this day.

When we got back to the house, my mother asked in her sweet voice, "You girls having fun?" Mona rolled her big brown eyes, saying nothing. Looking at my stubbed toe, I managed to say, "You bet!" We never told anyone about our near-death experiences that day. Mamma was so used to me looking roughed up because I was such a tomboy that she didn't notice the depth of my dishevelment.

Driving Fate

Mamma never learned how to drive an automobile, and our new young neighbor, Anna, who was sweet and gentle as a lamb but also a flaming feminist for the times persuaded my mother, contrary to my father's approval, that every woman should know how to operate an automobile. Strong personalities could sway Mamma because she just wanted to please everyone.

So it was a beautiful summer morning when my father was at DuPont that Anna backed our family car out of the garage onto the street and turned the wheel over to my mother. She steered slowly up the street, headed toward the river; when she made her first right turn—or more to the point attempted her first right turn; she didn't understand how to straighten out the wheel—panic set in and her right foot jammed the gas pedal to the floor, causing the car to leap and crash into our neighbor's house! The car ripped through the side of the house, driving over the kitchen sink and stove into the middle of the living room before coming to a stop. I witnessed this surreal movie from an upstairs window and began running and screaming toward the scene, expecting to find everyone dead! "Mamma, Mamma!" I called as I leaped through the rubble into what was left of our neighbor's house. My mother was picking up cinderblocks, tossing them, laughing like a demon, and saying over and over, "Oh what a mess, Oh what a mess!" I was horrified! She really scared me!

Thank God our neighbor was not injured physically, but the trauma showed in her eyes and her silence. Anna was collapsed crying, and I began shaking my mother to try to get her to show some remorse. All three husbands were called to come home from DuPont. When Mamma saw Daddy she collapsed and began weeping like a mortally wounded animal. I have to admit I was relieved to see her show some sorrow—it seemed more human to me. Later it was explained that she had been in shock and that was how she coped with the situation.

The accident put a lid on Anna's liberation goals for my mother and had a far-reaching effect on me. It turned out my little brother Scotty was in the back seat and experienced the accident firsthand. I couldn't see him in the car, so it was a shock to find him in the middle of the chaos. He later had the unfortunate luck to be in the back seat of Aunt Millie's Chevy along with me when she drove through a farmers' market stand in the middle of a hairpin curve on Route 60 when chenille bedspreads hanging on a clothesline completely blocked her from seeing.

Because DuPont High School did not have drivers' training, the only way a girl could learn how to drive was probably through her boyfriend. Most parents in the '50s didn't see the need for their daughters to drive. The idea that another female in the family should ever take the wheel of a car was reason for my little brother to get hysterical. For that reason I didn't learn to drive until I was 30 years old and lived far away from the mountain roads of West Virginia.

Purple and Green

I could see my home and the side yard from blocks away as I returned from school. I would wonder as I walked toward home if my mom had baked something and if the smell of cinnamon would fill the air as I approached the front door. And of course the smell of her homemade bread would make me start running! Her snickerdoodles, butterscotch cookies, orange cookies, and all Pomeroy recipes were the most welcoming treats! My mother was the baking queen!

The laundry, however, could become a bit dicey! Poets say in spring the juices of life rise, and in my mother's case the juices created a domestic artistic expression that was unique to the neighborhood.

And so it was for many springs, on a day to be discovered from blocks away when coming home from school, I would see the clothesline crowded with all my previously white or other light-colored clothes dyed either deep purple or forest green! I wish I had known about Buddhist prayer flags then. I could have told my friends the colors were something my mother did for world peace. With hindsight I think Mamma was just following Mother Nature's lead, adding new colors for spring to liven up the landscape. Certainly the looming edifice of the DuPont factory as a grey and smoky backdrop begged for a little color. Alas, no such explanation was possible, and I think our neighbors were so amazed that they just behaved like it was normal to dye all your clothes either purple or green in the spring

I didn't think my mother was different in any serious way at the time. But later when she stopped doing some of these unique things I found that I missed them. What replaced her efforts was silence and inertia; coming home to a dark house with mother in bed unable to function made me long for the purple and green days of past springs. The situation brought a sadness into my heart I couldn't explain and began our role reversals; she to become my child and I her mother.

An Open Door

Something exciting happened. I made friends with the couple across the street, who were very different from everyone else in Lower Belle. They did not have children. The woman, Lee Lee, unlike the neighborhood women, had a career outside the home as a banker and wore high heels and elegant suits. Her husband, Gene, equally noticeable and different from the neighborhood men, left each morning not to work in the DuPont factory but instead drove to Charleston where he was CEO of a company. Nothing about their lifestyle matched the neighborhood, and they kept to themselves. Everyone wondered why they even lived in Lower Belle. They clearly could have chosen to live in a better neighborhood. After all our streets were not even paved.

I think our friendship began when I knocked on their door for Trick or Treat and Lee Lee was offering only fresh apples and I asked her why. I was a major chatterbox who was not afraid to have conversations with adults. They would often invite me for dinner. I was treated like a grownup, and it was a marvelous diversion from my home life. Our little dinner parties raised the bar of expectations for dining for the rest of my life.

One evening Aunt Lee Lee and Uncle Gene, as I was asked to call them, announced that her niece, a young girl named Dian, was coming to live with them and that she was my same age, my birthday being October 3rd and hers the 23rd.

Dian was the sister I needed, and her arrival created a functioning family environment that was not possible in my own life. She arrived looking very sickly with one eye turned in that would require surgery later to straighten. She had blond pigtails that were thick with ribbons tied at the end. She looked sad and ill, but happily this would be changed in her new environment. I remember Aunt Lee Lee taking an entire suitcase of medicine that was for Dian and throwing it into the trash, pronouncing, "Good nutrition is all a child needs to be healthy!"

Dian too had experienced some family problems that made her feel separate from other "normal families," so we had much in common, and a friendship was forged that was very solid. Later friends would refer to us as the "Tombstone Buddies." In a stage show in high school we sang "We are Siamese if you please," from the Broadway show *The King and I*, and we brought down the house!

It became very normal that I should regularly live on both sides of the street, being in my own house with my parents and younger brother and being the chosen companion for Dian and experiencing a different life entirely with Uncle Gene and Aunt Lee Lee. The contrast of culture and expectations was enormous. I learned how to fit into both sides of the street but over time began to feel a stronger sense of matching one family more than the other. And alas, being with the Archibalds was where I felt most at home.

Lee Lee and Gene didn't change the way they lived their lives with the addition of Dian and now a lot of me. They came home in the evening and had martinis before dinner. They would serve we girls a Shirley Temple cocktail that was ginger ale and Grenadine syrup or in summer sometimes a peppermint stick stuck inside a lemon half to sip the juice. We felt very sophisticated!

Dinner was never before 8 p.m., and we had to have perfect table manners.

"Carole, would you care for some roast beef?"

"Yes sir, please," and Uncle Gene would slice the meat and place it on my plate.

"Would you like squash?" and so on, and Aunt Lee Lee served the salad from the wooden bowl she had rubbed with garlic and tossed with her homemade dressing. It was very elegant, and we would be expected to offer charming and amusing conversation over dinner.

Even with the profound influence of delicious Pomeroy food that my mother maintained, this was my first experience with what I understand today was a gourmet version of family dinners. Sometimes I would feel very guilty that I enjoyed myself so freely across the street and would come home and cling to my mother seeking without words her forgiveness. She, being the unselfish angel, never over the years made me feel I had let her down in my preferences but instead understood that her restless child needed what the house across the street offered, and I think she was glad for me.

The Archibalds brought a new world to my life with travel, education, and a country club kind of life. I would become an Episcopalian and Lee Lee and Gene my godparents. They decorated a very beautiful bedroom with twin beds and matching spreads and drapes for Dian and me so I could sleep over all the time if I wanted. Dian would cry some nights when I would announce that I wanted to sleep at home! I would cross the street into my dark house and later notice the candlelight burning from my godparents' windows.

I confess that over time I became more like the adopted daughter to Lee Lee and Gene. With hindsight I now know that my mother was languishing inside the hell of paranoid schizophrenia with bipolar personality swings. I am sure this had an influence on the choices I made. Frankly, I mostly coped by accepting her eccentricities. Her madness was fun when she was hyper, but when she would sink into the depressed Edith Mae everything that we knew about her disappeared.

It brought an unspeakable sadness into our lives, and we never spoke about it. It was like waiting for a long winter to end and the undying hope that spring would return and the smell of baking bread and the joyful Edith Mae could be heard talking and laughing once again. Funny how we would forget the dark days and be again surprised when the silence would return.

A Soufflé Waits for No One!

The lovely table that my godparents laid captured my passion. Lee Lee expressed all the classic attitudes of a French-trained chef: "Only fresh ingredients in season should be served." Uncle Gene, a gourmand and a fine cook in his own right, held the same sacred standards. The quality of our daily meals and the high esthetic standards of a beautifully laid table with good china, silver, and linen napkins and individual crystal salt dishes shaped like swans made every meal special. In winter Saturday night dinner was always a standing beef rib roast.

Sunday evening was roast beef sandwiches with salad, ending with cake and green tea. We dined lightly Sunday evening because after church Uncle Gene would fix a fabulous brunch of pecan pancakes, scrambled eggs, fruit, and coffee! Monday was homemade soup, and Friday's menu was always fish.

At age 10 I wanted to make a soufflé for dinner and Aunt Lee Lee was my tutor. I whipped the egg whites light and fluffy and gently folded in the egg yolk mixture with chopped spinach, nutmeg, and Parmesan cheese into a classic white French soufflé dish.

"Gently, don't disturb the soufflé," she instructed me with some urgency as my small quivering arms reached to place the precious creation into the hot oven. "Now Carole, the next thing you must understand is that the timing must be perfect!" She continued to explain that everything about the meal should be accomplished and ready to serve so that when the soufflé is taken from the oven it must be served immediately, "A soufflé waits for no one!" Lee Lee intoned imperiously. I have never forgotten her urgent lesson.

Of course she was correct and I did, with her help, have the timing be perfect, and so was the soufflé! It was the beginning of a lifelong passion for cooking that swelled along with my soufflé.

Although my mother was a wonderful cook, as was her mother, the extra efforts that Lee Lee and Gene expected seem to suit my need for daily events to be just that: an event! Cooking became the stage from which I could produce, direct, star, and expect applause at the end. It became a portal for exploration, as I studied all the world cuisines and tried to duplicate them. Theme dinners were my specialty and are still. The impatient soufflé taught me the lasting pleasure of serving fresh food and the joy it brings to my table.

PS: Always use equal parts of vinegar to oil in a salad, and don't let anyone tell you otherwise!

The Wrath of God?

Cross my heart, it doesn't sound right, but in all honesty I believe it was Dian's idea that we should attend a Baptist church service in Upper Belle (as the only Episcopalians in Belle, we were curious about our classmates who were Baptist). The plan was that we would attend a service and pretend to put our money in the collection plate but in fact keep it, sneak away from the church, buy candy, and then walk home to Lower Belle on the narrow berm of Route 60. It would be a two-mile walk and we would be very conspicuous—two young girls alone on the roadside walking by the DuPont factory. There was so little walking space we had to go single file. Usually our fantasies were acted out in plays we performed safely at home, so for us this caper was particularly out of character.

Oh what smug, happy charlatans we were!

The caper was executed with poise, and we were enjoying the horror on each driver's face as they passed us with a few inches to spare. Walking facing the traffic neither of us realized that Aunt Lee Lee in her Mercury came up behind us and very calmly lowered the driver's window and said, "Girls, would you like a ride?"

We both had enough sense to say. "Why yes, Aunt Lee Lee, please!"

It was all very polite, and my gut told me this was a charade we were playing. Especially chilling was her calm voice. "Carole, you need to go home. Your father wants to see you."

I crossed the street and with an animal's instinct quickly went to my bedroom and threw my Mary Jane peanut chews under my bed. "Carole—come in here NOW!" My father's voice was shaking. As I approached the living room he said, "Don't you ever, ever, ever do anything like this again," and began flogging me with his belt. He was in a frenzy of fury and was crying as he hit me again and again.

My mother ran over and tried to grab the belt, crying, "Daddy, Daddy, stop, stop," and he pushed her down to the floor. I took the opportunity to run into my bedroom and lock the door.

I crawled under my bed, crying hysterically until I fell asleep. Later I awakened; it was so still and so dark, but I sensed it was safe to get up into my bed where I fell again into a nervous, exhausted sleep.

Suddenly, the bedroom door opened and the ceiling light was turned on. Out of the haze of sleepy swollen eyes I see my dad and, my God, my Grandpa Stewart! Daddy had driven all the way from Belle, West Virginia, to Racine, Ohio, and back to bring a peace offering. My father's eyes pleaded his case without words; we each learned a profound lesson about limits and why they are needed. We never spoke again about that traumatic Sunday.

My dad—Poppa Moose—was not a violent man; it was the realization of what could have happened to me that made him snap—it was not anger but deep protective love. The paradox of the two acts—Mother intervening and being knocked to the floor contrasted with my dad standing contritely at the foot of my bed with his father—offers for me the final explanation, which is ultimately their love for me.

I was not allowed to see Dian or Lee Lee and Gene for a couple of weeks, but when my house arrest ended I took up my old habits, living in two different homes and worlds too. Aunt Lee Lee, I learned, had spanked Dian with a brush, but there was no retribution like the one I had experienced. Lee Lee several times laughed about how bizarre it was to see the two of us walking in our Sunday best beside the highway like we were strolling down Fifth Avenue in New York City. The incongruity amused her, and I have to say I got it too.

Cute Tomato

The lipstick obsession began with the first tube: Cute Tomato by Cutex. It was a fabulous true, perky red that smoldered but was also innocent. It was made for me! Because of this beginner's luck, my spoiled lips have demanded lipsticks of brands and shades ever since. By the time I was allowed to have a lipstick of my own, the tomboy Carole had taken a backseat to a more civilized young lady.

Dian and I were "hired" by Aunt Lee Lee to clean the house on Saturday so we could have a little pin money of our own. We each were paid two dollars. One dollar had to be put in a Christmas club at Lee Lee's Bank so that we had money for holiday shopping, and 50 cents was tithed to our Episcopal church. This left us each 50 cents for pocket money, or "mad money" as Lee Lee would say. We were delighted with the arrangement because we were not allowed to baby-sit or do other jobs teenagers did for money.

One Saturday while dusting and polishing Lee Lee's dressing table, I couldn't resist opening the middle drawer. Inside I found a flat, red box with the name Elizabeth Arden written across the top. Carefully I lifted the lid and discovered a fabulous collection of lipsticks, powders, rouge, and things I had no clue about or where on the face they belonged. What I did know was that this box held the beauty secrets of a well-turned-out woman, and I was going to stealthily observe and learn. I knew that Momma had no such middle drawer or access to such exotic cosmetics, and so this mystery of makeup was to be unveiled via Aunt Lee.

My secret life as a cosmetic junkie unfolded slowly and initially without much notice. This, I confess, added another dimension of pleasure. I also discovered exotic creams for the face in the secret drawer and began using them as well. I don't know what tipped Lee Lee off—suddenly one afternoon she took special notice of me for some reason and after close inspection and sniffing my face— the covert cosmetic jig was up!! She realized my lipstick color and scent of exotic crèmes were familiar because they belonged to her! I was in big trouble for snooping, and worse still for "borrowing" without her permission. She made abundantly clear that such permission would never be forthcoming. Lee Lee also went on to say in a threatening voice that if I continued to put so many different crèmes on my too young skin, I was going to cause a major explosion on my face!

I blame the cinema, all those beautiful women in the '30s and '40s films with their perfect complexions, rich, full, lush lips and luminous starry eyes. Couldn't a girl from Lower Belle, West Virginia, named after the actress Carole Lombard, have some glamour as well? Alas, thereafter I was forced to finance my cosmetic addiction with my allowance, which meant "Goodbye Elizabeth Arden" and "I'm back!" to dime-store brands.

The lipstick obsession has never left me. I have drawers of shades and don't believe I shall ever find one that is as perfect as the no-longer-produced, illicit blue red of Elizabeth Arden that belonged to the lips of Aunt Lee Lee and briefly mine.

Black and White

Aunt Lee Lee, a very trim, elegant woman, never kicked off her three-inch alligator pumps after a long day at the bank; she never said she had a hard day and wanted to rest her feet! She stood in the kitchen dressed in her New York City elegance, cutting paper-thin slices of purple cabbage and green peppers with the precision of a brain surgeon, her carbon steel chef's knife sharpened to perfection.

"Remember girls, only serve what is in season. Always rub your wooden salad bowl with fresh garlic before you dress your salad." I would watch her every move; she was a woman worthy of study. My eyes recorded the balance of freely poured vinegar and oil and the secret ingredient, a pinch of dry mustard. "Classic French dressing—it always works!" she would say, and I agreed. Another mystery unfolded and is how I have made my salad dressing ever since.

Aunt Lee Lee's sense of domestic organization was also worth studying. For example, each of us had two sets of sheets for our beds—one for the weekly wash and one to be used. We each had two sets of towels for the same reason, and additionally these were color coded so you never had to wonder if you were using the right towel. On Saturday mornings when a sleep-in would have been wonderful, Uncle Gene would come into our bedroom and announce with the flair of a Broadway tenor, "Rise and shine, girls! It's a beautiful day in Chicago!" as he pulled our bedclothes away to begin the weekly washing. Needless to say, we were not in Chicago! It was always a rude way to start the weekend.

Think about this: a husband doing laundry in the '50s! Aunt Lee Lee had all the chores distributed. She cooked all the meals except Sunday brunch, which was Uncle Gene's specialty—wonderful pecan pancakes with maple syrup and smoked bacon. Dian and I were allowed to have a little café au lait! We felt sooo grownup! Uncle Gene and we were in charge of washing up after meals while Lee Lee played the piano. Even though she was a thoroughly modern woman ahead of her time, the one domestic ritual she kept was to iron Uncle Gene's shirts. She easily could afford to have them done but would say, "I'm just grateful to have such a wonderful husband's shirts to iron." It was not lost on Dian and me that love could be manifested by food, a gracious table, and ironing the shirts of the man you loved. For years I even ironed my husband's underwear!

I learned from Lee Lee to have only black or white underwear kept in separate drawers. Her elegant underwear was another eye-opener for me and fanned my interest. I was raised on the dime-store "day of the week" panties with the day embroidered on them—black was for Saturday and of course, white for Sunday. I had not seen such delicate, beautiful lacy things to wear before and loved the idea that it was a secret under your clothes that no one could see! I realize now that Lee Lee's taste in her undergarments was the same as her salad dressing—it was French! And I always think of her when I hear "La Vie en Rose."

After the Ball

A beautiful, regal, black velvet evening cape was draped across my twin bed, a gift from Aunt Lee Lee. This was a proper wrap to wear over my gown for my first ball at the Black Hawk Country Club. I had never owned anything so lovely! This would be my social debut with all the social pressures: wishing to look my best, praying my dance card would have no vacancies, and lastly having someone wonderful to share the important last dance. My expectations for romance and intrigue could have made an MGM musical!

Lee Lee's sister Hilda had invited us to visit and accompany her daughter Nancy to this important ball. We loved coming to Galley Bridge and higher into the mountains to Black Hawk, a special tourist attraction in West Virginia because of the striking vistas. Aunt Hilda's husband, Uncle Meffie, was related to Hoagie Carmichael and with no training could play the piano just like him! We loved to sing "Oh Buttermilk Skies—I'm keeping my eyes out on you."

The evening was out of a dream—it was a social success; I had a thrilling first ball. My gown was a creamy silk and I felt like a princess but the cape remains most vivid in my memory. Lee Lee had said, "You can't wear an ordinary winter coat over a formal gown—it would be tacky!" I think she was right, and to this day I have my opera coat to wear for such occasions.

The next morning, swooning with happiness, I could hear the orchestra and see the handsome Georgia Tech student with whom I shared many dances. I could hear the music and remember the line, "You stepped out of a dream; you are too wonderful to be what you seem," and so on; such evenings are dreamlike. Thoreau said our truest life is when we are in dreams awake, I always liked the phrase, but now I knew what he meant!

Dian, Nancy and I were called down for breakfast. We grabbed our robes and Nancy offered her slipper because the floors were cold. I was the first to begin down the steep staircase when the slipper slid off my right foot, causing me to fall or rather fly down the stairs, hitting my head on the last step! Blood began gushing from the back of my head. I had ruptured an artery.

It turns out that the handsome Georgia Tech dance partner (also a star football player) lived next door, heard the screaming, and came running over to see what was wrong. He carried me to Lee Lee's car to be rushed to Montgomery General Hospital with my head all wrapped in bloody towels! Just as a priceless crystal goblet breaks, everything that had made the previous night perfect was now shattered! I was a terrible patient; the blood frightened me so greatly that I just could not stop screaming and crying. Lee Lee, who was always very emotionally collected, became impatient with me, and this made me more hysterical. The hospital had to sew my head up, and to this day my hair parts right down the middle from the top of my head down the back. No hairdo can stop my back part; I gave up caring years ago.

After that ball, hysterics were put permanently to rest. Now if I suffer a trauma I just become mute. All my screams stay inside my head; Lee Lee would be proud of her Anglican convert.

Hold that Note!

On road trips, Dian and I could sing nonstop for 500 miles and Aunt Lee Lee and Uncle Gene never complained. We sang ourselves all the way to Nags Head Beach in North Carolina for summer vacation. Last weekend I attended a live concert to hear the world famous soprano, Rene Fleming. As she swept onto the stage in a beautiful gown, it was most apparent that her beauty was not confined to her voice. As she began singing I was enveloped in her glorious sound.

I could hear tonal qualities that were familiar from something much earlier in my life, and then the recognition washed over me; her voice had a unique tone that I had only heard once before, a voice so clear, so pure and velvety—it was Dian's voice! When Dian would perform before an audience I was so moved by the beauty of her voice I would cry. Now I understand that my tears were also for myself because once she was discovered as a potential opera diva we never sang together again.

All the spontaneously bursting into song that had been our way since we were very young ended on a summer day when she returned from a session with her tutor, who was preparing her for an audition to a prestigious music conservatory in the fall. Somehow she began to sing, and when he heard her voice he said, "You have a voice like this and I am preparing you for a piano audition!" He insisted that she should instead audition as a singer, and he would teach her four arias for the competition.

No more bursting into song now. Dian had to save her voice, eating sherry tablets before singing to clear the vocal tubes. Never should she drink milk or eat dairy products prior to a performance. Long hours of vocalizations, "la la la la la la la, up a note la la la la la la la," climbing ever higher into a coloratura range like Beverly Sills and Joan Sutherland, who were at the peak of their singing careers. Dian had a natural singing technique and most importantly a tone that was luscious. She often would end her stage performances with the popular song "My Foolish Heart," and the audience would melt—it was an amazing moment to witness.

Dian and I always sang in two-part harmony. I was the harmonizer while she held the melody strongly, and I could with complete abandon embroider around her voice—it was thrilling. Everyone enjoyed our singing together.

We never discussed this change in our lives. It was a split that was inevitable, of course, but I do wonder now whether she, like me, hears our voices in duet. Dian carried the melody and so she owned the song, whereas without her voice I had no melody and therefore no song.

Dian was accepted into the music conservatory where they were sure she could become a Metropolitan Opera star—it was just a matter of discipline and time. Singing was to be her life and nothing else should be considered.

But fate had other ideas! When Fee (my nickname for her) came home for summer break after her first year at the conservatory she announced she would not return! She did not want to live the life of an opera singer. Aunt Lee Lee was devastated. To appease her it was decided that Dian and I would go to university together the following year. This way at least her education would not be postponed, and of course this was a fortuitous break for me to go to college. I had spent the previous year in Columbus with my Aunt Millie working at the Jeffrey Manufacturing Company as a data analysis clerk.

I was thrilled to be going to school and to have Dian back as my best friend. It would not restore our singing together, nor did she ever even so much as hum to herself. The lark would not sing—her talent had turned against her, and all the songs we knew were lost.

Sometimes I imagine Dian singing in an Episcopal church with her children in awe that their mom can sing like an angel. We have not kept in touch, and sometimes when I hear a glorious voice with that special tone I am transported back into the melodies of my past; it is a duet always.

Lasting Dance

I could have danced with you through all life's rhythms. Our connection so sweet and trusting, you twirling me feverishly with your fingertips, guiding me in a dervish-like spin that made my poodle skirt rise higher, higher, undulating to show the legs that matched your every step. Breaking apart we still kept our rhythm and returned to each other right on beat. No music could defy us; we were together, partners in the dance of life. Dizzy from gyrations, I would fall into your warm chest, resting my head and feeling the strength of your protecting arms telling me that this is where I belong; you were my private home where only we two could live. Our music played on and with long strides, short steps, spins, and dips; eye to eye, heart to heart, we were one.

I remember at high school dances friends would encircle us and chant, "Go JuJi, Go Stew!" It affirmed what we already knew—that we were meant to be together. It was never questioned or imagined that anything could draw us apart. So how did it happen that we lost step and each other?

A lifetime has separated us but the passion for living a joyful, hopeful existence that I learned from you has not waned. You were my youth, a perfect span of time, and when I hear our song

"My funny valentine, you make me smile with my heart," I still do smile at you across time. With my heart, I follow your lead, and in the ballroom of my memory, we dance on.

Charm School?

He rested his hip on a stool supporting his lack of stature, more of a Truman Capote body type. But he was the local Svengali, and to graduate from his charm school meant you were ready for the high and the mighty! Nothing could elude you; no, as a trained charm machine everything and everyone was at your mercy. With his certification you and your atomic charm could cause a meltdown anytime and anywhere; you, Miss Prissy Britches, could rule the world. Men would throw themselves under your precious foot to keep you dry!

I imagined going back to West Virginia and people whispering, "Is that the former Carole Elaine—my she has changed! Well, you know the story of the ugly duckling, Transformations can happen!" I would wink with my right, false eyelash and pucker my Joan Crawford glowing red lips, with lines way outside my natural lip line, and blow an air kiss from my spotless white glove and then drop my right hand down gracefully over my hip, turn, and with a professional model's gait walk away, leaving destruction in my path. Indelible definitely!

Beware Siren on the Loose—every delicious male take cover or be devoured! This charming little vixen is always hungry! Oh, and did I mention that my transformation included a real VAMP hair cut, asymmetrical with shining peek-a-boo and peek-a-bang hair over one eye adding a dimension of mystery that was immeasurable!

STOP the film! It is time to tell you what really happened. The General of Charm, also known as Napoleon Bone-a-part, was, I now believe, a sadist who loved to scare young women into insecurity. Charm school, his style, was a boot camp to break down a young woman into thinking she was a nothing and needed to be recreated by his godlike wisdom into an image that he would install. "A woman only exists in the eyes of the man who loves her!" was his convenient interpretation of 1950s propaganda.

In the second session he told all of us to line up against the wall with our arms above our heads and like a general inspecting his troops with a riding crop under his arm, down the line he strutted, punching each one of us in the stomach. I realize now that was the moment when I transformed into the warrior woman who has stayed in my soul to this day.

With my newly short-bobbed hair complete with spit curls that resembled the forked tongue of a snake spitting onto my cheeks, my black beret pulled at exactly the proper French angle over one eye, red scarf around my neck, and my sexy black suit, I reached out to hit him back! He pulled away with shock and awe, to use a modern phrase, and looked completely stunned as I went running out the door, which I then slammed!

I can thank this despot for unleashing me from the culture of puppet woman and giving me the freedom instead to ride off into the sunset a freed slave ready for the liberation the future would bring; ahead of the curve, if you get what I mean.

In spite of the deprivation of not learning how to be charming, I have managed to live a life full of charm! I am free to wear shoes that do not match my purse, chew with my mouth open, and tip my soup the sensible way to get the last swallow, i.e., pick it up and drink and so on.

The Emperor of Charm was the thunderbolt that pierced the false façade of putting on airs and opening the virgin spring of my own original charm, and for that I am grateful. Don't be looking for a Marlene Dietrich double—she left the building in a snit years ago! Only the scent of a real woman remains. Breathe deeply! AH.

Backhand

"No Carole, your penmanship is not correct; you must NOT slant your letters to the left—backhand is not proper penmanship!"

I tried to write the letters in the designated blocks, higher for capitals, with just the appropriate tilt to the right, repeating the letters over and over. Once I was out of the practice boxes, the demon backhand slant would overtake me and off my penmanship would bolt like a bull leaving the pen at a rodeo. I was helpless like the rodeo rider. I just held on and hoped I would land safely. Well, if safely meant passing penmanship, I was definitely only headed to the emergency room.

My mother, on the other hand, had picture-book penmanship. Every letter was exquisitely formed; it was textbook spot on perfect and beautiful. That is why, when I was going to university with Dian in West Virginia, I was very disturbed to receive a postcard from Mamma stating that she was very fine, except it could not be true. Her handwriting revealed tremors in each stroke of her pen, each word forced by a will that was heavy and out of control.

I was studying for final exams and didn't allow myself to really take in what this postcard was saying—I was used to Mamma having her ups and downs, but her handwriting had never looked like this. I forced myself into my studies and pretended everything was normal. This false state of well-being was soon shattered when a second postcard arrived with the same message, verbatim, and the same pained penmanship.

Something was terribly wrong. All my concentration on final exams vaporized. I had to know what was happening to mother. I knew that my father had left her for another woman and that she and my brother Scotty had moved to Columbus, Ohio, to live with her sister Millie. She was very devastated after 25 years of marriage to have her life completely shattered. But this tragedy had not affected her handwriting!

I phoned Aunt Millie and she told me mother had a nervous breakdown and was waiting to tell me after my classes were over. She gave me the devastating news that my mother had been committed to the state mental health hospital. Aunt Millie had no idea that Mamma had or could send any cards and was sorry I had to learn of her situation in this way.

In 1964 I too moved to Columbus and had Mother released into my care to have her reevaluated. It was the beginning of the revolution in medications to help mental patients. Meanwhile, my mother had received 25 shock treatments and the hair over her temples had been burned off. Her short-term memory had also been affected. Shock treatment seemed brutal to me, but it was considered the best option at the time for paranoid schizophrenic patients.

Her illness had clearly begun during my childhood, but we were clueless. The sad fact was that no real treatment was available at the time. Mother's personality would change many times over the years—sometimes she thought we were sisters, or girlfriends—and it was not until the last few years of her life that Edith Mae came into her own with the help of lithium and I could see what her life could have been had she been born later.

Today I look at old shopping lists mother wrote, and I treasure her handwritten cookbook. It was a small victory when she regained some of her beautiful penmanship. In the chaos of her illnesses that tossed us about relentlessly, she would roll her eyes and say, "This life and the fireworks!"

I still write backhanded and am grateful that this remains a contrast to the perfection of my mother's penmanship where my mother is the winner, hands down!

Destiny

As I boarded the train, I remember clutching my white straw hat with a navy blue ribbon that matched my navy and white linen dress with a white Peter Pan collar. I had two suitcases and my Samsonite hatbox that Julius, my first love, had given me as a Valentine present when we were in high school. I was traveling on the night train to Washington, D.C., for a summer job.

This summer adventure was made possible when, on a dare, Dian and I and some of our college girlfriends took the civil service exam in Charleston for summer jobs in Washington, D.C. It was particularly risky given we had been in evening gowns dancing at the May Ball the night before. We were really tired the next morning when we took the test. We screamed in disbelief as our individual telegrams arrived saying we were hired for the summer and should report to the main navy building on Pennsylvania Avenue in early June.

Now the trick was to convince Aunt Lee Lee and Uncle Gene that we should be allowed to go off to a big city together without adult supervision. After some major begging and promising to stay in a highly recommended residential hotel for young ladies, we were told we could go; but never were we to go out unescorted at night etc., etc., etc. I remember the gleam in our eyes as we agreed to all the rules. Whatever it takes, we thought, we are going to the nation's capital. YES!

Dian and the girls had traveled to D.C. a week earlier, and so I was taking the overnight train to arrive just in time to report for our job assignments. This was a dream come true for me; I had said I would live in the nation's capital since I was four years old!

My overnight train would arrive around 10 the next morning at Union Station. Dian and the girls had given me the address for the cab driver. An admiral and his wife, who were also going to Washington, D.C., invited me to join them for dinner in the dining car, where we enjoyed a wonderful dinner with white-glove service by candlelight. They were amused by my rapture over a summer job in D.C. Trains were a wonderful way to travel at the time.

I sat upright all night watching the dark shadows rush by the window and keeping a protective eye on my luggage. My heart was racing with anticipation when the train arrived at Union Station the next morning. I had never taken a taxi, ever! Because Uncle Gene had stressed how crime-ridden D.C. was, I was determined that no one should steal my luggage and carried each case out walking sideways so I could keep watch at both sides until I had made it safely outside to the taxi stand.

When the taxi pulled up to the address I had given him, the place looked nothing like a residential hotel for young ladies. It was, in fact, a row house on Woodley Place that I would later learn was famous for its summer residents; a book had been written about the street.

Dian and the girls came squealing out the door, and we all screamed, hugged, and jumped up and down the way excited girls still seem to do. "Is this the hotel we promised to stay in?" They all looked down and then began laughing. No, it was not, and it would be our secret. Of course we would be corresponding with Lee Lee and Gene, certainly no phone calls would be made in those days, so they figured we could have real freedom, and Washington was not a bit the way Uncle Gene had painted it. I was escorted to my room where Dian and Mary Jane would be as well. Three twin beds were lined against the wall.

That Saturday evening I had my initiation into life at Woodley Place; everyone opened their doors and parties were in every house, and all the young people who lived on the street were roaming house-to-house, party-to-party. Being shy and tired that first Saturday I opted, if you can believe it, to stay in my room and read a book.

Soon there was a knocking at the door and a very tall, handsome, athletic young man with black hair whose name I would learn was David said, "Hello. Welcome to the neighborhood—I will introduce you to everyone." He swept me off my bare feet, up into his arms, and off we went into the street.

When my escort needed his hands for getting a drink or whatever, he would hand me to another guy, where I stayed safely aloft until he returned. I met every person on Woodley Place that evening, and my rather lofty social position was established! It was well after midnight when David gently returned me into my own row house, the first time my feet had touched the ground that entire evening. It was a great initiation.

The sexual revolution and the birth control pill would not come until decades later, and there was an innocence and sweetness that I wish I could capture for today's young people. The summer of '59 was to be one that would place me into another life. Little did I know in the June of that summer that I would never return to West Virginia or the life I had known for 19 years.

Destiny II

After my arrival into D.C. the previous Saturday, Monday morning brought the initiation into what would become my future. Dian, Mary Jane, Joan, and I reported to the main navy building on Pennsylvania Avenue at 8 a.m. sharp, having successfully used the city bus system! We had never lived in a city, and it was exciting and stomach churning at the same time. A large room was filled with young ladies, and as they alphabetically called out names everyone received her summer job in different governmental agencies. My friends, all earlier in the alphabet, were assigned to Housing, Home, and Finance—I assumed when they got to the Ss I would be as well. I was quite wrong! I was the only person in the room assigned to the Joint Chiefs of Staff in the Pentagon—across the river in Virginia. I was so disappointed! It meant taking different transportation, being on a different schedule, and parting from the day-to-day experiences of the summer with my friends.

I had to transfer buses in front of the State Department to cross the river to the Pentagon. I could not have imagined what would be ahead for me. I just knew the Pentagon had five sides. I was mustered in as they say and placed inside a very small windowless room with a desk. I was told to study all the documents and understand them before I could "join my team."

Why would the government waste a month to prepare me for my summer job? I had to learn flag rank, the grades of generals and admirals, and military protocol. Plus I learned what they called standard operating procedures (SOP) so that I could implement the training of the crème de la crème officers who would be serving in the JCS. I was afraid to say, "But I just came for the summer—I am going back to university in the fall!" I then learned that the government was spending a fortune for a security clearance that would place me in the same category as the president of the United States! It came as a major shock that I had been hired for a full-time position.

The first day I was placed with my team in operations, President Eisenhower's son was in my office, the handsome air force general head of NORAD, along with my team of officers, and I was so overwhelmed I stuttered every time they tried to talk to me. They thought it was quite charming and soon took me under their wings as a daughter. Hence I got over the trauma of change and was actually able to function and do my job very well.

As we all learn in time, fate can be preparing for our future without our realizing it. And this certainly turned out to be true for me, because my summer job in D.C. turned out to be my future. In August, Dian married her high school sweetheart, Glenn, who followed her to D.C, and we were both disinherited. Lee Lee and Gene had high hopes for Dian and her talent, and the thought of her marrying anyone at the time was obviously unbearable. I was devastated by their blanket rejection of us both. I was not allowed to even go home to gather my clothes. My future education and the rest of my life were tossed away by these people whom I had loved so deeply. It was a painful adjustment and probably left me with fear of abandonment to this day.

Fortunately, the education I would receive at the Joint Chiefs of Staff would be incredible. Being in Washington, D.C., when John F. Kennedy was elected president was so exciting you could feel the high expectations in the air. Mother nature became so thrilled she dropped one of her biggest snowstorms in the history of the city the night before his inauguration to mark the occasion. Stranded people hung out in hotels and bars and celebrated all night. I began to realize that I was not just experiencing history, I was going to be part of history! This was a gift I could not have wished for myself. My horizons now included the entire world – quite a leap from the West Virginia parameters that had formed me.

My metamorphosis began in grief but the butterfly that emerged was a quantum leap forward. No looking back! My future was mine alone to achieve. Circumstances forced me to become an independent, strong woman determined to stand on my own.

Like smoke rising from its source of fire, I too had to rise and find my own form and learn to say with a strong voice: "I AM!"

Thanksgiving for One

As you learned in Destiny II, in August my godparents disowned both Dian and me when she eloped with her high school sweetheart Glenn. Amazingly, my summer job, through some twist of fate, was in fact a permanent job, unlike my college mates who returned in the fall to the university. Of course that was my plan as well, but it was no longer possible.

The Woodley Place summer was over, and I took an apartment with a new roommate, Mary Jane, who was very sweet and as innocent about life in the big city as I was. We moved into a one-bedroom apartment on Connecticut Avenue that was one of the smaller buildings, and we lived on the fourth floor. It was a great location. In the zone we lived, a cab ride to Woodward and Lotherps, Hecht's, or Garfinkles cost 50 cents. My commute to the Pentagon was shorter, although I still had to transfer, because I really worked in Virginia.

Mary Jane I both planned to catch a ride with some friends to West Virginia for the Thanksgiving weekend. She would spend the holiday weekend with her family—I planned to visit my high school sweetheart Julius and his family. It would be the first holiday I would spend away from my godparents.

I was 19, and everything I knew as "home," a place where one can always return, no longer existed.

When you work in J3 operations in the Pentagon you can image how stressful the days can be with matters of national security. As luck would have it, I was unable to leave early and missed the ride home. Mary Jane had caught her ride, and so this is how I had my first "Thanksgiving for One" in Washington, D.C.

Mary Jane and I were very afraid of the man who supervised our building. He was always finding reasons to use the key to come into our apartment. He would have an excuse, but we felt his motives were not pure, shall we say. Mary Jane, who was a big, beautiful woman, would answer the door with a large butcher knife, holding it with a firm hand and pretending she just happened to be chopping some vegetables. He always brought our mail up, which was not necessary or appropriate. And so you can imagine how I felt about being in the apartment alone for four days.

I had never spent a night alone in my life. That evening I pushed furniture against the door and quite honestly was afraid to go to sleep. Mary Jane and I were not very good about saving money for food. Truth is we depended often on our dates to be the source of dinner. Otherwise we mostly lived on scrambled eggs. I can remember always buying fresh flowers from the lady on the corner even if it meant no food. I know you know where I am going with this. I didn't really have anything in the apartment to eat for Thanksgiving, and everything was closed. We didn't have a television or a radio. It was 1959, after all.

I decided to read *The Diary of Anne Frank*, a book I had recently purchased from Brentano's bookstore in the Pentagon. I was so swept away by the diary and the emotions and hopes of this young girl that I forgot about Thanksgiving and the apartment and fell completely under the spell of this young, brave girl. It was a crying marathon too.

The minute Thanksgiving Day was over, the regular rhythm of life returned and picked up where it had paused. I felt better. I had survived two nights alone, and I was not dead.

No, I was alive, unlike Anne Frank, and this recognition made a change in me that was equal to a conversion. I needed to breathe fresh air and walk the streets; unlike Anne I was free to live! I was going to live for Anne too. I would never be alone again.

I went with this new attitude to the Episcopal church a few blocks away, taking my Book of Common Prayer that Lee Lee and Gene had given me upon my confirmation with the inscription, "With much love and good wishes always." The general Thanksgiving prayer we always recited by rote came alive, "Almighty God, Father of all mercies, we, thine unworthy servants, do give thee most humble and hearty thanks for all thy goodness and loving kindness to us." I felt the joy of a mystic!

The rest of the weekend was a joyful adventure that included my going to a beautiful Japanese (Yes, Japanese!) restaurant. I was seated on a silk cushion on the floor with a lacquered black table. A warm moist napkin was placed in my hands, and I felt a warm glow grow throughout my body. I had never experienced such food, so elegantly served with new flavors and taste sensations. I drank the green ten and wondered what my godparents would have thought about this experience I was having. I realized that I was finding another level of gourmet dining. I really began to understand how much more there must be to experience in this city laden with international delights. Adding to this unique pleasure, a handsome young naval officer in his dress uniform toasted me with his teacup and kept smiling at me from another table. I thought I was Madame Butterfly with a happy ending.

On Sunday I went strolling way down Connecticut Avenue and happened upon President and Mamie Eisenhower walking up the stairs to their Presbyterian church. I just followed them in and enjoyed the service looking at the back of their heads. After all he really was my commander in chief!

When Mary Jane returned with her Thanksgiving stories I was thrilled to have her back with me in the apartment. But I knew, even if she did not, that I was not nor would ever be again the same roommate she left on the previous Wednesday and my "Thanksgiving for One."

Daddy Love

In the movies in the '30s, '40s, and '50s children were usually obedient and courteous to their parents. The relationship between the father and the daughter could be particularly sweet; the darling girl could just wrap her daddy round her future wedding finger. I believe it was called acquiring "feminine wiles." It seems harmless enough, the art of persuasion little girls absorb early on.

Of course, the little girl does not know she is playing a role to acquire power, something she will badly need for her adult life and the battle of the sexes. So where is the behavior learned? In my young life, the movies were good instruction for the art of dealing with daddy. After all, he is another species entirely—so primeval instincts were activated.

My daddy was mostly a mystery man who was usually away. He looked very handsome in his DuPont factory supervisor's shirt with a tie, a windbreaker, and most impressive, his hard hat. He really resembled the actor Robert Mitchum except for the dimpled chin. Poppa smelled nice and was fastidious about his body; he even shaved under his arms, and I think it was his Tussy deodorant that I associated with his scent. His eyes were green with flecks of gold. Both his parents were Scottish. Mary Scott and Walter Scott Stewart had three sons, and my dad, the first born, was named after his father. Like him, he loved to drink and hang out in the American version of pubs.

Not really getting much time with my father I look back and realize much of my dialogue with "Poppa Moose" (an endearing name that came from nowhere except me) could have been a movie script with young actress like Judy Garland. "Oh Poppa, may I, PLEASE, Oh Poppa, I PROMISE!" Also, the shared memory of his beating me with a belt because I had done something very dangerous when I was younger scared us both into the idealized father-daughter dialogue. It was a safer script for us both.

Our detente lasted until his death. Recently I have wondered how much he had affected my life. I don't recall ever being embraced by him or kissed by him, but I do remember how it felt to have his attention, his eyes showing amusement and pride sometimes. And I was allowed more freedom than either my mother or my brother, Scotty. He showed no signs of resentment toward our neighbors across the street, who became my godparents and made a room for me in their home, raised me to be Episcopalian, and took me away for summers to Nags Head. He knew I was learning a different way of living that would separate me more and more over time from my mother and him.

When he left my mother and she and Scotty had to move to Columbus, Ohio, to live with her sister Millie, I hated him. I was living in Washington, D.C., and felt so guilty that my brother had to leave his high school and Mamma was being tossed out like a candy wrapper after 25 years of marriage. I, too, was devastated and refused to have any contact with my father for over a decade.

It was only after my mother was diagnosed as a paranoid schizophrenic and placed in a state hospital for the mentally ill that I was finally able to confront how her illness must have affected their relationship. I moved to Columbus, removed mother from the hospital, and had her medications reevaluated. But even with medication it became clear to me that day-to-day life could never be normal, and I began to realize how much her illness had to have affected her marriage.

Slowly my anger began to melt and the ice in my heart regarding my father began to thaw. I began to understand why he had relinquished me to my godparents—to give me a better life. It was an act of love and sacrifice.

I decided to travel to Charleston to visit my father, and I had my first real conversation with him as an adult woman. We had candid conversations, and it was clear that he felt very guilty about mother but just could not handle her illness. She went untreated until moving to Columbus. He thought she was in a better place, and that was true. No treatment would have been available in Belle. It was a time when mental illness was considered unfortunate but no rehabilitation was expected, only hospitalization until you died.

We went to dinner at a restaurant where my dad was a regular, and as we were leaving some man at the bar said, "You're robbing the cradle, aren't you, Pops." My dad slugged the guy. You see, he was a lot like Robert Mitchum!

Daddy married twice after mother. His second wife died of cancer after two years of marriage. He remained single for many years and then married a shrew of a woman in South Charleston, the ritzy side of town, who was just a gold digger. Shortly after the "I dos" he moved to Florida but stupidly never divorced her, so when he died she received his pension instead of my mother.

Years before his death he made peace with my mother and would come to Columbus to visit all of us. In the last few years of his life, before dying of cancer, he and my brother, who also lived in Florida, formed a close relationship, and in the end Daddy was able to feel the love of his original family.

Forgiveness is a very healing response, and I am glad that he was not alone at the end of his life with no familiar face to meet his final gaze.

Poppa Moose does live on in his only daughter. Like him I am restless, always wanting the road less traveled, can't be bored, drive fast, love my car, and mispronounce words. My ear doesn't let me know, so my mistakes are a family joke that continues. Differences: He loved to hunt and would bring home his kill for mother to cook. I cry over road kill. Daddy's handwriting was small, precise, with perfectly formed letters like a scientist. I write backhand with unbalanced letter formation and live in the other side of the brain. But I know we are connected, and part of him has made me the character I am.

The most important lesson I learned from the relationship with my dad was the power of forgiveness. It washes away hate and pain and leads one onto the forward path of resolution.

Daddy's ashes went out to the sea where he loved to fish. Returning to the ebb and flow of nature, I hope he has enough action to keep him content.

Thank you Poppa Moose for bringing me into this "Life and the Fireworks" and for your green eyes!

Lilies for Louise

The tar black night upstaged a subtle moon. The moonlight was pale and tentative, its white spheres of light anemic. Perhaps it too was sad with what was imminent: the death of Louise. She in the height of youth, beauty, and intellect was to be taken from us. We also were young, and it was too soon to suffer such a loss. We were frightened to the core. How shall we live without this beacon of grace and wisdom? She was always wiser than the rest of us. She occupied another dimension and understood what were mysteries to the rest of us. Louise truly had an aura that drew people to her and they stayed.

Studying in Europe, Louise adored being a student at an Italian university in Perugia, where she loved riding her bicycle down a steep hill where the local policeman would blow his whistle to stop the traffic so she could coast through the intersection with her long Swedish blond tendrils flowing like Botticelli's Venus. Her golden topaz eyes flashed with happiness, and she must have felt immortal. She wrote letters home, and we hung on every word. It was a vicarious life with Louise that made us dizzy with joy and anticipation.

When the letter arrived that a lump had been discovered on her arm and the doctors were adamant it should be surgically removed immediately we were sure she would be fine. Another letter arrived saying they needed to remove her arm, and later the most horrible news came that her right shoulder was to be removed because of cancer.

She joked about her cat being confused. He had liked to sit on the missing shoulder but now had adapted to sitting on the left.

Of course we had begged that she should return home with the first letter, but she didn't come home until after the shoulder amputation and the news that the cancer had taken over her entire body. She would be coming home to die.

Louise's bedroom became our sanctuary, and many of her friends came from Europe to stay with her literally until her last breath. We had wonderful evenings of sitting around her bed having great conversations, laughing. It was a perfect salon. Gertrude Stein would have been envious. Her body swelled, and gallons of liquid would need to be drained for her comfort. This would require an ambulance ride to a Boston hospital. She endured every discomfort without complaint.

Her example made each of us strong, and we only wept far away from her presence. I believe she was more concerned about each one of us and how we were going to adjust after she was gone. I, a new mother, was coping with a failed marriage, but I hadn't said anything about my unhappiness. I only wanted to be strong for her. The night before she died she asked to see me alone. She took my hand and said, "Your unhappiness I can hear like cathedral bells pealing. You must leave this marriage and be strong on your own." I cried so hard, I couldn't speak; I just moved my head up and down in agreement and finally rested my head against hers.

Around midnight, her friends and I decided we would gather water lilies from a pond we had seem earlier that day for Louise. We were all afraid; it was so dark, the moonlight not approving as we each entered the black, cold pond, our feet sinking into silt. I imagined we would be entangled in the long lily reeds and drown together. Perhaps fate understood how unfair it was that Louise should die the next morning and some retribution should be extracted.

We arranged the beautiful white water lilies all around her bed, on the tables, everywhere, lilies and candlelight. You cannot imagine how truly mystical and reverent was the tableau; our exquisite Louise surrounded by beauty that was worthy of her, and the love in the room was palpable.

My grief over the loss of Louise was unrelenting for two years. I did leave my husband, her brother, and I raised my child with the help of my beloved mother and Aunt Millie. I wonder if Louise knows how much she altered the path I have trod since the night of the water lilies. Now when I see exquisite lily blossoms upon the water they reflect Louise's beautiful face, glowing saint-like, surrounded by holy candles, and the cathedral bells toll this time proclaiming my freedom.

I Hate Santa Claus!

Christmas was coming and I would be facing the holidays as a single parent. Moving to Columbus was the right thing to do for my son Rob. He would have family around him and feel part of the tribe I call mine. I had taken Mother out of the hospital, and with the new medications she could function at home, where Rob gave her a reason to live. They became great buddies. He also had his Aunt Millie to dote over him too. He really had three mothers, an abundance of riches.

The "snoop sisters" as we called Mamma and Millie, provided an excellent environment for Rob as I needed to find a job so I could support us. My job in the Joint Chiefs of Staff in Washington, D.C., had paid an excellent salary, but moving to Ohio meant starting over. The difference in salaries and attitudes moving to Columbus was alarming. We were, at the moment, pretty much living at the poverty level. I would come home from interviews stunned by such comments as, "You would be bored here," "You are too qualified," etc., etc.

Fortunately, the personnel director at The Ohio State University did not see me as a lost cause and I was hired on my first interview. This began what would be a wonderful career and restoration of a living wage and more.

However, this Christmas I did not know the future and was feeling very sad. I decided I would take Rob to see Santa Claus, determined that he should have this traditional holiday experience that I personally never had. Lazarus Department Store offered a special breakfast for kids and then a chance to sit on Santa's lap and give him your Christmas wishes. When Rob sat on Santa's lap I was a little worried about what he might be wishing for but decided it was worth the risk.

The energy to propel me through the holidays had come strangely in a dream. It changed my attitude completely—from feeling helpless to feeling confident! In the dream I grew taller than the Christmas tree under which Rob sat. And from that image, I profoundly understood that I was no longer the child under the tree but the mother who must now create the magic for my own child. It was like being born again but this time as an adult who would take pleasure in her responsibilities. I will never forget this dream. I believe it saved me from having a sad life.

But, of course, my reverie did not spare me frustration. Certainly after shopping for Robby's presents and learning that everything needed to be assembled I was really put to the test. I spent the entire night before Christmas with screwdriver in hand trying to put together a million pieces of a Hot Wheels racetrack. It seemed impossible! I had bloody fingers, and at one point the fatigue and frustration got to me and I had a good cry.

Finally I had arranged everything under the tree, with packages to unwrap and the Hot Wheels racetrack in the middle of the floor so that when Rob came down the stairs he would have an exciting view of what Santa had done for him.

Now I knew why parents looked so tired on Christmas morning; I was exhausted but equally excited to see the expression on Rob's face when he saw and felt the magic of Christmas in Columbus.

The moment could not have been more perfect. He was wearing his little flannel pajamas with feet, and as I led him down the stairs I waited for his reaction at the dramatic moment! It was very dramatic but not at all what I had hoped. Rob looked very puzzled and then sad, with no happy face for his Hot Wheels. Nothing! "Honey, what's wrong?"

He looked up into my eyes and said, "Where is the washing machine?"

I replied, "What washing machine, sweetheart?"

"The one I asked Santa to bring you!"

I have hated Santa Claus ever since.

Lady Queen

"Momma, wear this dress, I want you to be the prettiest mom at the PTA meeting." Rob, my son in the first grade, would stand beside my dressing table and watch me apply my makeup, observing every move of the eye-shadow brush. "No, Mom, not too much. I want all the kids to say you are the prettiest mom." He insisted I should wear my blue dress, and he figured my long, black hair would be the critical attribute to move me into the league of "Top Mom." The pressure was pathetic on my part.

Although I had helped my friend Dian backstage compete and win beauty pageants, I had never been a contestant. For starters I was exhausted from working all day, my feet were tired, and a nap would probably bring out my questionable outer beauty more than any makeup. I had never anticipated having to compete with other first-grade moms who were, I supposed, under equal pressure from their kids. But maybe not, maybe this was just a Robbie J. thing; me following his script—after all, children do completely change your life's scenario.

Rob always had ideas about me that felt like I had been cast as the star in a movie he had written and was directing. His curiosity about me had no competition,

I was washing dinner dishes one evening while Rob played in the backyard with some friends when suddenly he sprang through the back screen and reached under my dress. His little hands were about to pull down my underpants but were intercepted by my soapy hands in the nick of time. "Mom, I want to see what you got!" Honestly, how many of you mothers had a similar experience with your sons? Do not answer.

Rob wrote wild descriptions of me in his school papers. His teachers always eyed me with suspicion! He wrote and told people I was a witch; actually he did ask me if I was one and I did say, "Yes." He seemed very pleased. Heck, why ruin the fantasy! I figured I was paying forward with some extra power on my side that would be needed later.

He wrote that my real name was "Moon Dog" and that I had special powers when the moon was full.

Although I had been considered an excellent cook for years, he wrote that I made terrible meals for him! He loved my ricotta fettuccine, a dish I made up for him with his favorite lemon salad. He adored avocado with fresh lime juice and an omelet as a before-bed snack. I would take him to the gourmet section of the Lazarus Department Store at the end of the month when money was short and allow him to choose food and put it on my Lazarus charge. Rob always chose the same exotic cheese imported from France that I now realize was a goat cheese wrapped in a large chestnut leaf tied with hemp. It was basically a glorious cream cheese, and he loved to eat it with fresh pear. I was proud of Robby's sophisticated palate and knew how unusual he was in this regard for a grade-school child. And so when I would get that special look from his teacher I would play along and chuckle under my breath knowing that Rob and I shared a little secret. You could put a smiley face here!

So many indelible sweet memories of Rob as a child, but one is particularly unique. He would approach me with reverence, taking my hand and looking sweetly into my green eyes with his huge blue eyes and thick black eyelashes that should be against the law for a boy, and place a plastic ring from the bubble gum machine in my hand, saying sweetly, "Mamma, here is some Lady Queen jewelry for you!"

And so it has been a major pleasure for me to be Rob's real and imagined mother and most especially to be his Lady Queen.

Driving in Time to the Music

"Elaine, I know you can learn to drive! I will teach you!" said my new best friend, whose name was also Carole. The dean's secretary at The Ohio State University introduced me to the College of Pharmacy by my middle name because I was the third Carole she had hired. Without forewarning I became Elaine, a christening without water that would symbolize my new life in Columbus, Ohio. It was the middle '60s and the world was on fast-forward, so putting my foot on a gas pedal to keep pace with the culture seemed like a risk I had to take.

Carole did not know of the many traumas I had experienced regarding the automobile. On a hot summer evening at Nags Head, North Carolina, where my godparents vacationed each summer, I was accompanying our young friend, Archie, who was driving their family maid home. I was sitting in the front passenger seat. Archie stopped in front of a store, for what I can't recall, and left the car engine running and the driver's door open. As he was about to enter the door, the car began rolling forward toward the store's plate-glass window.

I, who knew nothing about cars and driving, was suddenly facing the equivalent **of going** over Niagara Falls. I began screaming: **"Archie,**

Archie!" He turned around and when he saw what was happening began screaming: "CLUTCH! BRAKE! GAS! CLUTCH! BRAKE! GAS!" over and over. I was clueless—his commands meant NOTHING to me. I looked back at the maid; her speechless mouth was wide open and her eyes were as big as 120-watt light bulbs!

Archie sprinted to the car, reached into the open car door, grabbed my left foot, and slammed it onto the BRAKE. The car stopped just in time to NOT hit the storefront plate glass window. We all looked smaller afterwards. I don't believe I ever saw Archie again.

So how could Carole—this tall, blond beauty, knowing nothing about me—be so sure I could learn to drive an automobile? She also knew nothing about the crashworthy driving histories of my mother and her sisters—the buildings driven through and the mayhem without murder was the mystery. Drivers' education didn't exist when I was in high school, and some girls compromised their virtue to learn from their boyfriends; a little trading of favors, shall we say. With the exception of my mother and her one spectacular attempt to learn to drive described in an earlier cupcake, her sisters continued their daredevil car-driving exploits behind the wheel until old age.

After being stopped in her 80s for driving on the wrong side of a boulevard in the neighborhood where she lived, Mother's oldest sister, Millie, threw in her keys and never drove again. Her 1964 Chevy, however, lived on to become the backup car for everyone in the family. The car always started in bad weather and, like Millie, never let anyone down. Actually it was horrible to drive; it floated around the highway like a barge that had drifted away without its captain. The steering wheel screamed every time you turned at any speed. But that battleship of an automobile repeatedly saved many of us until 1993 when Aunt Millie moved in with me and sold the car to a local collector. Amazingly, I occasionally see it being driven and the year is 2007!

Feeding on Carole's confidence in my ability to drive, I made the New Year's resolution to earn a driver's license. I told her, "I always kept my resolutions."

She said "Great, we will begin your lessons after work in the parking lot." It was January and snow had been plowed into piles; my first driving lesson would be in a field of white. I touched the steering wheel with the fear of meeting an alien force.

We graduated to my actually driving on real highways and making, gasp, left-hand turns. Every maneuver was a miracle. I just couldn't believe a person could place her hands on a circle of leather, press a pedal, and have access to every inch of this country—amazing! I also took lessons from a professional driving instructor so I could receive a lower insurance rate should I ever afford a car of my own.

"Don't steer off the edge of the car," my instructor would call out. "Eyes always far ahead and then back and forth between the rear mirror and the side mirror." Over time I began to feel what Carole called the "rhythm" of driving. She handled the steering wheel like a concert pianist and drove with such grace it was like watching a thrilling performance. I so admired her ease with this lethal machine called CAR and was determined to become as brave at the wheel as she.

In March I passed my driving exam. BINGO! I am a licensed driver. Determined to make a new history for female automobile drivers in my family, I would balance caution with courage when behind the wheel. I think fear makes for a bad driver. Aunt Marcella was a rabbit gasser when she drove her big Buick. She would tap the gas pedal, lunge forward a few feet, stop, hit the gas, and hop forward again. It was like Peter Cottontail, hopping down the bunny trail.

Aunt Julia, who had no sense of braking distance, was constantly running into the back of stopped cars waiting for red lights. My dad, on the other hand, drove like a professional race car driver, wrecking several cars but never injuring himself or others.

Carole and I decided we would celebrate my becoming a licensed driver by driving cross-country to San Francisco in July using our vacation time.

We took turns driving; she was much better on mountain curves—a driving rhythm that was more at the master's level of steering, which I had yet to cultivate. I have a photograph of Carole eating tuna out of a can while standing on the sideboard of the car. We were in the desert outside of Las Vegas and afraid a rattlesnake would bite us. We used the roof of the car as our table. The previous day I had driven over 100 mph into Reno. We figured it was safe because there was nothing to hit on either side or other cars on the road.

But the greatest experience was when we drove across the San Francisco Golden Gate Bridge; it was so symbolic. Two girls from Columbus, Ohio, had driven across country! We were so proud, plus the film *The Graduate* was very popular and one of the great scenes is when Dustan Hoffman drives across the famous bridge to the music written and sung by Simon and Garfunkel: "Here's to you Mrs. Robinson, Jesus loves you more than you will know, ho, ho, ho ho, ho, ho." Windows down, wind blowing our hair, singing at the top of our lungs; it was magic! We were the stars in our own movie! We crossed twice, each taking a turn at driving across so we could both say we did it!

It was amazing to experience the varied geography of our country. We drove the northern route west and the southern route to return east. The experience was life changing, and what a great gift my friend Carole gave to me. She always said, "Elaine, you will be a natural; you will drive in time to the music," and she was right. I do.

It was the only time I was Elaine in my life, and I enjoyed it immensely. All these years later, when I, Carole, start my engine and press my foot to the gas, Elaine takes the wheel and we turn on the radio.

California Dreaming

When Carole and I decided to drive to San Francisco, we had no experience traveling, and one of the pharmacy professors who was from the golden city on the hill suggested that we stay in the Monroe Residential Hotel. I was particularly reassured when I saw an advertisement for the hotel in *The New Yorker* magazine.

Crossing the country, we stayed in many different hotels or motels. In Salt Lake City we arrived later than we had expected. We had not made reservations ahead because we weren't sure how far we would travel each day. We had gotten stuck behind a terrible truck filled with dead cattle in the back, and the smell nearly killed us. Plus it was a two-lane mountain road and passing was impossible. Thus, we arrived after dark into the city.

Lady luck had taken the night off. "NO VACANCY" signs flaunted their tongues in neon colors as we drove endlessly, seeking a place to rest. It was beginning to feel rather biblical. Finally exhausted, we decided to take a room in a motel we had earlier resisted because it was the exact replica of the motel in the film *Psycho*. And much to our horror the very strange young man who could have been Norman Bates from the film was apparently the only person who worked there. The room was small and cluttered and uninviting. Carole and I really felt we were being watched and were afraid to go to sleep. I can still recall vividly the paranoid weariness. We were so relieved to not be dead in the morning and agreed that showers were definitely out of the question. After Salt Lake City we made reservations ahead in the Great Western hotel chain, which seemed to be always consistently nice, clean, and safe so we could feel more secure about where we lay our heads.

Don't get the impression we expected to be living first class; we were on a very small budget for such an adventure. We saved money by eating canned tuna and buying fresh fruit from roadside produce stands. It was before bottled water, but we did manage to keep something to drink, and I can't recall having ever an emergency regarding water. We were very careful crossing the desert; we prayed the car would not break down. This was before cell phones and you hoped if you had an emergency you could rely on "the kindness of strangers," as Blanche Dubois would have purred.

After crossing the Golden Gate Bridge, we had no trouble finding the Monroe Residential Hotel, but parking became a problem. A man who lived across from the hotel offered a space under his apartment building and we were set! PURR!

The person who came out of the hotel lobby to assist us with our luggage was rather exceptional; he was wearing rubber boots unbuckled and a heavy winter coat and it was summer and not raining. His hands were completely covered with warts. Carole and I felt another Salt Lake City "Oh, no" moment and began laughing. As he and Carole, along with her luggage, crammed into the small elevator, I said, "Never mind. I will walk up." Carole gave me one of those "Elaine!" looks as the door closed on the two of them, and I deserved it.

The hotel was far from posh, but we were thrilled to be in this dream of a city. We had adjoining rooms and it was only 40 dollars for the week and this included dinner! It was a steal. I said to Carole that I hoped the fellow who helped with our luggage would not be serving dinner too.

We went down into the basement that evening for dinner, and sure enough here he came bringing our first course, a cup of soup, with his lovely warty thumbs resting inside the bowls. "You first," I said to Carole.

That night just as we were about to fall asleep all sorts of wild screaming and running began outside our room in the hallway. Apparently a game of touch football had been organized by some of the guests on our floor and they seemed to be high on something else besides football.

It was a tense first night, but after a bit we just relaxed with the culture and felt very lucky to have a hotel we could afford.

When I look at the pictures from our trip my favorite is of the two of us on a cable car. The driver stopped the car so he could take a picture for us. How sweet was that! Another is of the two of us by the sea, Carole, tall, blond, and windblown, and I the brunette, short, in a fisherman's sweater and a polka-dotted mini-skirt I had purchased for 50 cents in a second-hand store.

Carole and I did not have a single argument throughout the trip. And I have never met to this day a person more clever and witty than she. She was a delightful "comrade"; I believe that is what we called one another. Carole left her heart in San Francisco with a young man named Mike, who broke it after we returned, and so her memories of our odyssey will be bittersweet, but for me it was all sugar. Upon my return, my boyfriend said I looked very skinny, "You have lost weight on the trip," and fixed me a ham and cheese sandwich. I was very grateful it was not tuna fish, our road food for weeks!!

I shall always recall Carole and our friendship and wish everyone had such an adventure to remember. We would sing, "Those were the days my friend, I thought they'd never end." But of course they must as we grow into wives and mothers and move into the spiral of this life and the fireworks. However, to this day nothing excites me more than the phrase "road trip!" I can be in the car in a New York second!

Créme Queen

Every day begins with the same ritual learned early in childhood from all the women in my family: immediately after bathing, apply wonderful lotion! I reach for my beloved body lotion and rub it over every inch of my skin. To be bathed in moisture makes me feel like a set of kid gloves throughout the day. It is the same secret that wearing beautiful underwear gives to a girl's attitude. No one else need know, but you feel special and act differently because of it. The ritual is a confidence booster and sends a little message: you are worth it!

Now the face is another territory entirely to be approached with reverence. As a child I watched my aunts gather in the bathroom and, taking turns, each dip her fingers into what looked liked congealed water that stuck to your fingers like Vaseline. They said all the movie stars used it so it had to be good! It was called Abolene Cleansing Crème.

My aunts had such a good time. They laughed, and I believed it was a sacred girl ritual I wanted to learn. I secretly began slipping in afterwards to rub this greasy crème into my very young skin. Not realizing the crème was to be removed, I left oil slicks on my grandmother's starched and ironed pillowcases and was very quickly exposed as an underage addict to Abolene.

Little did any of us, and certainly not I, realize at the time that this addiction to crème on my face and body would never be diminished but instead would grow into an obsession that by now could probably moisturize the entire earth with several applications. When I travel by air, I always carry on board my crèmes in case my luggage should be lost. Clothes, shoes, etc., I can live without, but crèmes NEVER!

At age 19, living in the nation's capitol, I found Garfinkels Department Store and it was crème heaven! I still get a rush when I walk into the cosmetic department of any upscale store. Why? Because they carry crèmes from around the world. Oh my God, the promises made are so achievable: You only need this crème! Hey, I believe it. I feel sorry for girls who don't crème; who let Sister Age push them around!

I loved Polly Bergen's turtle wax foam, which was a frothy, light pink and smelled very like lemonade. I used it until Polly apparently ran out of turtles. I was very panicked at first, but just like life, another crème came to my rescue! Jacqueline Corcoran, the famous female aviator before Amelia Earhart, came out with a crème that was so luscious I didn't know whether to eat it or put it on my face. It looked like French Vanilla ice cream, a rich yellow, and smelled like crème brulee! I am sure I moaned with pleasure as I applied it to my face.

The next morning I awoke to see 60 blemishes covering my face! When I saw the dermatologist he said I was far too young to use such a serious crème on my face that was made for a very mature skin. Well, that did set me back for a bit, but then I found Clarins and used it for years until they changed their formula. I then fell into the arms of a Shiseido representative named Joy, who mothered and fed my crème addition for nearly 25 years.

I remember my godmother's warning when I would mix dime-store crèmes purchased with my allowance and slathered onto my face at bedtime, "Carole, someday your face is going to explode from all the incompatible chemicals you are mixing on your face." My unspoken reply was, "Woman, you are a coward!"

Because Shiseido has become too expensive, I am out seeking and testing crèmes again. Presently I am trying a Dior, a Lauder, a lotion a dermatologist mixes himself, a little Olay, and a French Olive Crème, plus a few that I can't remember.

I will tell a crème, "No, not this morning, I will use you tonight," so they don't fight in the cupboard while I am gone. I also have the crèmes organized by shelves and placed so I can find the right crème in the dark by touch alone. This is important because when I get up to go to the bathroom at night I always reapply some face crème.

However, I do suspect some mean spirits coming from my cupboard today because of what happened this morning. I am newly out of the shower; my hair is askew, covering my eyes entirely. While listening to the BBC, I reach for my presently favorite tube of body lotion and begin rubbing it into my feet, ankles, caves, thighs, up and up to the neck, and then some cleansing crème to my face.

I comb my hair and begin to notice that my entire body is beginning to stiffen and my skin is feeling very strange. I go to the cupboard to check which crème I had applied and with the gift of sight discover that my John Frieda hair slick crème had found its way down from the third shelf for hair products to the first shelf, which is for body crèmes. And the tubes feel exactly the same! I had applied hair slick all over my body! I had to throw myself back into the shower!

Needless to say, the John Frieda hair crème has left the building! I have freshly applied the right crème and now can slide through the day as usual.

A beautiful model told me her secret to entering a room full of strangers: just say to yourself, "I am beautiful. I have a secret. Everyone wants me!" I have adapted this to, "I am clean. I am creamed. Now make a scene!"

Curry and Spice

Flying over New York City, recognizing buildings like chess pieces: the Empire State Building and the Chrysler Building, with its pointed chapeau crowning itself the tallest of tall for a while. The Statue of Liberty, as mysterious as the Mona Lisa, gives me a wistful look. Does she know how very far I will travel? Twenty-four hours later when I would land in New Delhi, India, it would be 2 a.m., the sun resting, leaving the city dark but her presence like a woman's perfume lingering, the city's skin still hot.

Stephen, my husband, would meet me at the airport, and our mutual dream of being in India together would begin. He had prepared me for the first impressions, the smell, the heat, the kinetic energy of so many people; it could frighten a Western-bred person. He had told me about his first experience of landing in India many years before to teach in Varanasi. He had traveled with some other scholars, and the first impressions had been so overwhelming that several of them booked a return flight to England, having never left the airport.

When the plane's engines stopped, the sauna-hot air of New Delhi quickly began to seep in like hostile, moist fog and the fuselage began to hiss and fill with opaque white smoke; I thought we were being gassed! In fact we were being fumigated—no Western insects allowed. The combination of fatigue and feeling like a sprayed mosquito made me light-headed when I deplaned. Stephen found me quickly and extracted me from the sea of people. Outside the terminal, I drew in my first breath of India. The air had a thick, sweet aroma of rich honey with an undercurrent of smoke and bug spray.

The dung fires were the source for the honey-sweet smell. Who would think dried cow pods could be transformed into perfume? When fresh manure is spread on farm fields in Ohio, few would say it smelled sweet.

Our taxi sped through the crowded streets, and we arrived at the bed and breakfast that was well known by European expatriates. The floors, the walls, everything was marble and offered an illusion of coolness.

Being a very practical traveler I had filled my suitcase with bottled water and many packages of cookies I bought in Zurich. Stephen and I are both great cookie lovers, each raised by mothers who always kept a filled cookie jar. It was an offering of the familiar, reminiscent of home. We laughed and talked and soon realized that it was morning and we had eaten all the cookies!

We joined the other guests at a long community table for breakfast. A young Indian cook made fresh wheat chapattis on an electric cooking ring. Being a rather wild cook, I had never considered tossing raw dough onto a cooking ring. They were delicious! I was very impressed.

A young, bright, and engaging India scholar from Cambridge was an immediate friend, and I loved his name, Crispin! A rather acerbic, unshaven American scholar named David gruffly acknowledged our presence. One suspected he preferred the company of people who knew nothing about his research in India.

He eyed Stephen like a competitor. We learned that his wife was in the hospital, having gotten very serious food poisoning in Kashmir. Her husband seemed more amused by her distress than concerned, as if it had been a contest and he, the stronger, had won. We soon learned from Crispin that he considered David a cad of a husband. "He had no business taking Kathryn to Kashmir and letting her eat mutton!" Crispin said with anger in his voice.

A young French woman and major drug addict seemed an escaped cast member from the Mad Hatter's tea party from *Alice in Wonderland*. Most of her face, which could have been nice, was below the tabletop, and she held her coffee cup eyebrow level as though she could drink from her eyes.

She had a cigarette burning down to the flesh of her fingers, which were stained a deep, brownish yellow. Occasionally she would surface, chin above the table, to make an inaudible remark. Apparently the French drug addicts loved to be in India. At night the other addicts, who never came to breakfast, or any meal for that matter, were activated by the light of the moon and never appeared in the harsh light of tomorrow.

My infatuation with India began as a young girl when I discovered Mogul paintings—portraits of beautiful women and men with extraordinary eyes reaching around the corners of the face with large black sapphire pupils. The figures were arranged in exotic dress in lush gardens.

Now these exquisite figures had come to life, stepping out of my dreams into the brilliant light of reality. Queen Victoria of England named India the "Jewel in the Crown" of the British Empire. It would not seem an exaggeration!

My habit of washing my long hair daily was a problem because the slim pipe carrying water into our bathroom did not have enough pressure to really rinse out the soap. Stephen suggested I go to the British hotel for a proper wash, and it was a delightful experience that had nothing to do with my hair. No, instead I had the opportunity to watch an Indian bride being prepared for her wedding that evening. And the attention to her appearance was an education. Her very long hair was set with orange juice cans, two ladies were using pumice to remove hair from her legs, and a henna artist was drawing elaborate patterns on her palms. She was very stunning, even during her transition. Meanwhile the hotel was preparing a flower path of marigolds the bride would tread to the marriage platform covered with flower garlands where she and her future husband would sit.

We returned that evening to have dinner at the hotel as an excuse to have a peek at the festivities. It was better than any red carpet Oscar night in Hollywood. Mercedes' doors opened to guests dressed in silk saris and gold jewelry that would not be possible in the Western world. It was breathtaking! As night fell, the groom arrived riding a stately white horse, looking every inch a prince. The groom was from Rajasthan, and this was their wedding tradition. As we walked back to our residence, we both said it was like a scene out of "Scheherazade." The dazzle index was way past anything you could imagine.

The next day Operation Jacob and Nancy began, a major undercover project in which Stephen and I, to this day, find amazing that we actually agreed to play our central parts.

Really it came down to an act of affirmation. We believed the charade we were about to perform was to serve a greater good. It was to make possible the marriage of Jacob, our dear friend from India who had received his PhD in the United States and wanted to marry an Ohio girl with whom he had fallen in love. The problem was that Jacob, a newly graduated doctoral student, was major marriage material for his family, and the dowry he could command would in turn create an excellent dowry for his sister.

Our task was to pose as Nancy's parents and to convince Jacob's large, extended family that Nancy was in her own right a woman of worth with a master's degree and therefore had the long-term capacity to contribute money to the family. If she and Jacob could be married with their blessings, the two of them would give money for the sister's dowry, and the family's investment in Jacob's education would not have been for naught. Basically, Jacob was worth around one hundred thousand dollars on the arranged marriage market because of his education.

When we arrived in Jacob's village, everyone was either on their rooftops or lined on both sides of the road to welcome us. The sight of Nancy with her blond hair and skin as white as milk beside the mahogany handsome Jacob caused quite a stir. It was as though we were royalty. We had tea and fried bananas and began the bargaining. I became an art history professor, as Nancy's mother, and Stephen could be himself, a history professor, except for pretending to be Nancy's father. Actually her parents were divorced, and traveling to India on such a mission for them was out of the question.

That evening we had dinner at a very long banquet table where all the family members were seated. We toasted everyone and did our best to make a good impression and to persuade the family of Nancy's worthiness as Jacob's bride. We went to bed that evening with mixed emotions but again thought our friends deserved their chance for happiness.

The next morning we learned the marriage had been approved!! We left the village in a state of euphoria and guilt. The good news is the marriage is a very happy one with three children and Jacob has a major position at one of the most prestigious universities in the United States. We are bound to them forever because of the "mission impossible" we shared and succeeded in accomplishing.

That the devil was in the details seems to sum it up. Now it was time to return to seeing India, and Stephen had arranged a driver to take me to see the Taj Mahal at sunset.

All my life I had dreamed of this.

Sun Burned

The sun has treated me the way a cat treats a mouse, slowly and stealthily aiming for my demise. It is fire that gives the sun its glow and its temper! Pale-fleshed beings are particularly easy prey. We who match that description are brainwashed into believing that we must have a suntan to look healthy. To be beautiful we need the sun's glow on our cheeks for a summer fashion statement. Pale is out; golden is in.

The brainwashing was very prevalent when I was in high school and college. We mixed iodine and baby oil and slathered it over our flesh. Iodine dyed the skin upon application, so it was very encouraging. My sorority sisters and I would climb out onto the sorority house roof with this emulsion applied and hold silver reflectors to motivate the sun to come, come closer. We were so dedicated we would suntan between classes.

One of my earliest assaults from the sun came on a mild, cloudy, overcast, windy day. I fell asleep in my Aunt Millie's garden while reading a book. I awoke hours later and felt very dizzy and sick to my stomach. I thought I had come down with the flu. I staggered into my aunt's kitchen where a large mirror hung over the sink and saw I was not red—I was purple! I looked like a burn victim.

The pain was horrible for a solid week; it felt like someone was ironing my skin, and anything that touched me was unbearable! Over time I began to peel, deeply; at one point I reached for my earlobe and all the skin came off my ear.

The sun has tried to bring me down in more subtle ways as well. When I marched for the Equal Rights Amendment in Washington, D.C., in 1978, we marchers were lined up alphabetically by state. Ohio came much later in the afternoon; we had been standing in the hot sun on the mall since early morning. The great feminists of the time were speaking on Capitol Hill: Betty Freidan, Bella Abzug, Gloria Steinem, and Marlo Thomas, to name a few. It was very thrilling to be part of this important event in feminist history. By the time we had marched to Capitol Hill it was four o'clock in the afternoon and I was feeling very weak. I left my delegation without saying anything and ended up fainting among strangers.

I had sunstroke! When I finally awakened and was steady enough to be on my own, I couldn't find my friends and didn't know the phone number or address of the home where I was staying. This is before cell phones. I was bunking with several well-known women from Ohio, including Mary Miller, the godmother of the ERA in Ohio where the referendum had passed, and the governor's wife. This information made it easier for me to be returned to my friends like a lost child. They had been hysterical and searching for me everywhere. Mary had to laugh later when admitting that, strangely, her first call for help was to her husband Bill back in Columbus. And some men think we flamers don't need them.

When visiting Key West with friends I had the idea that I wanted to ride a bicycle literally around the entire island. Although my bicycle was old fashioned without gears and my friends were riding more travel-worthy ones, shall I say, I thought I was doing just fine keeping the pace, etc., etc.!

My friend Michael kept turning around and asking, "Are you alright?"

"I'm fine!" I wondered why he kept watching me! Finally he insisted we stop and get some water. I was quite shocked when instead of offering me water to drink they poured the water over my head! Steam rose from my body and I sizzled! I was a human oven! We headed back to Michael's beautiful conch house on Elizabeth Street where Elizabeth Taylor's former in-laws, the Burtons, also had a home. When I saw myself in the mirror I understood why I was scaring everyone. It took hours for me to return to a normal shade of pale.

I don't sweat—literally, it turns out—and my body temperature gets so hot you could fry an egg on me. The sun knows this can be lethal and has tried multiple times to GET ME! Other incidents have occurred since that deadly tango between the sun and me, but so far I have kept cool by the light of the moon!

I am known as the midnight gardener. I do everything at night that others do in the light of the sun. I watch them sweating outside from the cool inside, I wonder why? I recommend instead a little hide and seek from the sun. It is a cool sport!

I Can Eat Anything!

Mamma proudly pronounces as she pats her ample tummy. She looks at skinny me with pity. Of course nothing could be further from the truth. In fact, my mother is a serious type-two diabetic, but in her present state of mind no such threat entreats her daily bread.

She stands before me in one of her famous Hawaiian-style muumuu dresses in pastel blue that matches her bright cornflower eyes. In her present state of mind, we are sisters and she likes to recall our childhoods. Because I have heard many of her stories before, I can play my part in her fantasy.

I wear my skirts long, and in a creative attempt to mimic me, she has cut fabric from her bed sheets and whip-stitched them to her hem. Even better, she has adorned all of her frocks with handkerchiefs pinned on by many brooches. I love it when she is so happy.

In the middle of the night I smell one of her delicious apple pies baking and the sweeper running. She adores housework and does it when the rest of us are in bed trying to sleep—it is her time to rule the domain completely. She is the Queen of the Night and worthy of opera music by Mozart.

Coming downstairs for breakfast it is always fascinating to see what the night as wrought. Mamma may have wound all the loose string into a knot or cleaned our kitchen drawers and cupboards and rearranged everything. Opening the cupboard door reaching for a glass, you get a skillet! The silverware is rearranged, and finding a spoon could be a tricky morning challenge. The apple pie, it turns out, is a pear pie and tastes even better than made with apples. She is the only one who can make Pomeroy bread like her mother Bessie Shannon. If ever you wanted to convene a meeting of all our family alive or dead, just release the aroma of Pomeroy bread baking, and in seconds be it from heaven or earth all would appear around the table. Aromatherapy indeed!

Although Edith Mae's world is small, she creates adventure within the rooms of her home. Her vacation spot is in the basement where she does the laundry and ironing. She has a lawn chair covered with a beach towel and her beloved radio that plays elevator light classical music. She can spend hours in her private resort and return upstairs to the kitchen with the excitement of one who has returned from a great vacation and sees everything with new eyes.

Actually Mamma's idea of a QE2 trip across the ocean is to go to her favorite Big Bear grocery store. She powders her face and applies a light touch of lipstick and earrings to match her dress. Her hair is arranged into a high chignon on top of her head, which gives her a semi-regal appearance. Also, she gains several inches of height with this hairdo, bringing her up to a full five feet.

The minute she clutches the handle of the grocery cart she is off like a horse in the Kentucky Derby! Butter, half and half cream, chicken livers, codfish, rump roasts, pineapple, lots of milk—she loves milk! Baking ingredients, chocolate, marshmallows, and walnuts begin to fill the cart. She also sneaks treats like Little Debbie Cakes and Payday candy bars. I pretend not to notice. Fresh fruit for pies, and peas, her favorite vegetable, which she always creams.

When we get home and unload all the groceries she offers me a glass of her famous ice tea. This is the only time she behaves like a diabetic. She puts every sugar substitute invented into her tea. It is a chemical cocktail that defies description and leaves a normal person shaking after a few swallows. After a visit with "Pebbles," his nickname for Mother because of her Flintstone hairdo, Reverend Hal from the Methodist church would roll his eyes and say he was recovering from Pebbles tea.

Mother would relax on the sofa, reclining with one knee bent that she constantly kicks back and forth, or she would fling one of her arms tirelessly back and forth—this perpetual motion could only be ended by doing housework, laundry, and cooking.

Sometimes this energy would take a left turn and trouble would be the result. She climbed on top of my son Rob's desk to get a key to unlock his closet where he hoped his possessions would be safe from her famous charity—give always. She had, after all, given away our dining room furniture and our clothes one day as a surprise when we returned home. Well, fate decided in favor of my son, and sadly she fell and broke her leg.

In the emergency room at the hospital Mother was her usual cheerful self when her energy was so hyper, and we sang hymns as we waited for the doctor. I tried to tell the physician that mother's accident was a result of her manic stage, but after a psychiatric evaluation he who had completely fallen for my mother's sweet smile said, "No," that could not be the reason for her fall.

She had the same magical effect on her regular physician and would bake sweet rolls to take as a present for him. "So, Mrs. Stewart, how is your blood sugar?"

Mamma would look into the doctor's eyes with her beguiling blues and say, "Just fine, around 80." I would start choking at this point. Of course this bare-faced lie would quickly be revealed by checking her blood sugar, and it would be 300!

Oh, but did I like these little sweet lying times the best. The flip side of Mamma was total silence, no expression, a darkness and distance that separated her from everything.

Suddenly the "I can eat ANYTHING" stage could return like a beautiful sunset. In the middle of the night the aroma of something very delicious baking and the returning hum of the sweeper would be the most beautiful and welcome night music of all.

Come Home Right Now!

My mother's voice on the phone at my office: "Come home right now!" I was so frightened I didn't ask why. I just slammed the receiver down and ran out to my little Fiat car, which had a sensitive disposition but seemed to understand that I needed the throttle, the clutch, and the gas pedal to cooperate and allow me to speed my way home!

I rushed into the house expecting awful news; instead my mother was smiling more broadly than usual. "Look," she exclaimed with great enthusiasm. Had she won the lottery? Had she inherited an estate, perhaps a castle in Scotland?

Without ceremony I grabbed what turned out to be a Polaroid snapshot of a rather elaborate gravestone. It had a marble vase carved into the middle of the headstone, sort of like a decorative separation between twin beds. The stone was already inscribed: "The Fisher Sisters: Mildred 1908- and Edith 1916."

"All you have to do is have our death dates carved when we are gone. We have already paid for our cremations and the headstone. You don't have to worry about anything when we die. You can even send our ashes UPS if you want to!" Mamma exclaimed.

I had to sit down, I thought perhaps my son had been injured or Aunt Millie had died. They had just sent their last payment paying off the headstone and felt very excited about owning their hereafter. Had the sisters been imbibers, we would have clicked our champagne glasses and toasted: Here! Here!

Mamma died on the 14th of March 1991, but I kept her ashes thinking she would rather go with her older sister, whenever that should be. Aunt Millie lived with me and was 93 when she died in 2001. On her birthday that year she announced: "This will be my last birthday!" and she was right. My mother had done the same thing, announcing her departure in two weeks, and she departed right on the last day. I was impressed.

I have the sisters in matching marble urns, and many friends offered to go with me to the Pomeroy I have so idealized in my stories to the beautiful old Beech Grove Cemetery. We would put the sisters to rest side by side near their mother, father, grandparents, and a brother. It was a stunning autumn day and all the trees were full of the finest fall colors. This cemetery was completely romantic with its rolling hills and old trees filled with the artful headstones from other centuries.

We walked and walked and searched and searched and did not find the headstone. Finally the search was called off and the sisters and I returned to Columbus, where they still remain! The present year is 2008.

Periodically, I am very concerned about the breach of their burials. I have honored their presence by placing them on a window box with a sculpture, candles, and flowers. One friend wondering why I have such frequent trouble with things electric suggested it is Mamma and Millie showing their pique with me for not getting them to their proper burial site.

Quite by accident a friend's wife, who has a passion for solving genealogy mysteries, took on this challenge. Dian and Stephen began going to Pomeroy on their own, examining records and researching my family. I have learned so much because of them. I have letters handwritten in German, obituaries and a wealth of information. The cupcake entitled "The Lottery" could not have been written were it not for these delightful super sleuths!

Most amazing they called to say they have found the Fisher sisters' headstone!! They had taken colored pictures, and it was an awesome headstone. The problem was that, for reasons I shall never know, the sisters bought burial sites in Chester, Ohio, instead of going to Beech Grove. This is the town where American Electric Power built a nuclear plant and has since paid all the occupants to move because of the high occurrence of cancer! And moreover, towering over and directly behind the Fisher sisters' headstone are the nuclear stacks.

Oh God, poor Mamma, it is like going back to the pollution of the DuPont plant in Belle, West Virginia. For this reason I have been incapable of taking them to bury in this deadly environment. I have no idea what to do. Meanwhile, my phone often does not work, my computer and television are down frequently, and the lights keep going out! Maybe my friend Ruth's theory is right. The sisters are upset about my not following their explicit instructions. Ruth believes that if and when I should take them to Chester for burial all the electrical problems will end.

However, at the moment it seems electricity and I shall battle on until I too am dust. I want to be tossed off Jockey Ridge on Nags Head Beach in North Carolina so I know where I am headed. Shall I take the girls with me to blow in the wind by the sea or leave it to my dear son Rob to continue the dilemma?

Okay, let's take a vote!

Something's Wrong with Your Nose!

Lowered expectations regarding me are my destiny when it comes to my Lebanese friend, Joseph, whom I call the "Leb." He calls me "Foot" because of the Blackfoot Indian blood I have swirling in my DNA from my grandmother Stewart. No, I can't tell you how this can be true. I never doubted the story because my grandmother could have easily made central casting with her high cheekbones, almond eyes, and black hair, which faded very little even in her 80s. Perhaps the best proof for me is how, after just a few swallows of wine, I look fried. Low alcohol tolerance is very much an Indian thing.

The Leb has saved my life a few times, so that helps to explain why we are still friends after 20-plus years. He performed the Heimlich like a trained medic one evening at dinner, saving me from choking to death (REALLY); he pulled me back forcefully from stepping out into traffic in New York city (NO JOKE); and most recently he discovered that I had forgotten to turn the oven off when a sudden power outage from a severe storm happened in the middle of baking. Joseph came by to check on Miss Kitty on the fourth day of the blackout, and while petting the cat smelled the burning cake in the oven. So once again by turning off the oven I am in his debt for saving me -- this time from another bout with my nemesis, fire. Yes, all the above is true, and NO I am not "an absent-minded idiot!"

Yes, he has needed a little help from a friend over the years and I have been there for him, but gratitude is not an emotion he flaunts, and I am fine with that. Actually I enjoy our Mexican-standoff culture. He tried to teach me how to play a game called Rock, Paper, Scissors. Apparently everyone in the world has played this game except me! The minute he started the game, I just started laughing like a loon and pelting him with unstoppable sissy slaps! He shook his head with disbelief and repeated how we are supposed to show either rock, paper, or scissors. STUPID! I just ignored his instructions. What a stupid game! Of course, I always insisted I won. It is one of the few times he is left "speakless," as our Bavarian friend, Christian, would say. I rather enjoy his silence.

We flew to New York City to see a major art exhibition at the MOMA some years ago. We got off to a rocky start when the Columbus ticket agent insisted that we had flown the day before! I had to pull one of my famous "Anna Magnani fits" to get her to reverse her decision and allow us to board. Joseph seemed to be siding with the ticket agent, never passing a chance to be on the "au contraire" side of me.

Arriving in New York we checked into the Salisbury Hotel off Fifth Avenue where we had a "suite" that included a kitchen and was very spacious. As we were just getting settled in and I was applying lipstick, my well-documented compulsive habit, I happened to look out the small window in the front door and noticed that emergency lights were flashing in the hallway. "Joey, come look. Something weird is happening."

He looked and turned, "The hotel is on fire. We have to get out now!" He swears that I looked into the mirror to check my lipstick before I responded, "Let's go."

I was sure that he was lying about the mirror thing because I never look in a mirror to put lipstick on; everyone knows this except him, apparently.

We raced out the door, leaving everything behind, and began descending the stairs. We could smell and see smoke. We followed some sweet little old ladies down from the sixteenth floor. It was great to get outside. "Let's go to the Plaza and have champagne while our things burn." He agreed, and off we went to the Palm Court. So you see, sometimes our minds do work in sync, and that is how our friendship survives. Oh yes, the fire in the hotel was quickly extinguished, we were told upon our return. It would not have surprised me to have seen a message written in smoke on the mirror: "Sorry to have missed you. Get you next time!" Signed "FIRE!"

Joseph met me at the airport once standing nonchalantly holding a big sign that read CRONE. I am eleven years older than Joseph, and he does love to rub it in.

We both enjoy all the arts and occasionally will go to the symphony together. One perfect July evening as we left the concert hall we admired how lovely was the indigo sky with a full moon and a cool breeze. To cap off this fine evening we rushed to one of our favorite restaurants for a late dinner and glass of Prosecco.

Pleased that we had made it just under the wire for ordering, sitting happily at the grand old-fashioned marble bar, I noticed that Joseph was paying very close attention to my face and looking deeply into my eyes. Very strange, I thought. "WHAT?" Given his gaze, I expected possibly a rarely given stingy little compliment like, "I sort of like your hair tonight."

But instead I heard, "There is something wrong with your nose!"

"You are such a six-year-old!"

"Good grief!" And we both begin laughing so hard we could have fallen from our bar stools. These are the moments that continue to cancel our "final day" arguments and hang-ups on the phone.

We both are students of the ridiculous, and insults are just juice for the next contest.

Joseph tries to tell me how to dress, fix my hair, NOT use lipstick, and decorate my home, how to treat my cat, how to plant my flower garden, and what I should do with my time when I am not with him. Amazingly, we always agree on politics and music.

I find it amazing that he always thinks he has the upper hand and has won all our arguments, when I know for sure it is the opposite! Just like the Pink Panther and his houseboy who enjoyed plotting the other's demise, we thrive on the challenge of competition in a rare form of friendship.

Yes, Joseph, I know you will demand I rewrite this, blah, blah, blah; read my hands! This is MY book.

PS reader: There is something wrong with my nose!

Making Carole

The assembly line was over-taxed. It was 1938, and the criteria for making humans seemed to be getting more complex. Apparently the Hollywood movie industry in the United States of America was making the prototypes more and more demanding. No one has ever seen these noble personages who have the awesome responsibility of assembling us for birth with special specifications. Maybe the Oxford University scholars from Great Britain who study antiquities by examining garbage from ancient digs will someday find the first scriptural references to these noble employees of the Parts and Assembly Department for human beings.

Can't you picture it? Ears in one bin, noses in another, teeth, feet, sexual identity parts, hair, lips, and toes—it is mind-boggling! I think they were under extra stress when they assembled me; perhaps the factory knew WWII was coming and made more girls because the boys would not have an equal chance to flower as grownups.

This mother admires Carole Lombard. What do you think? Maybe she really admires Clark Gable!

Well, we don't want to make an Appalachian girl have a mustache and a gravelly voice; she would need to go to Berlin or New York!

No, this one needs to be, I think, a mix of a little Bavarian, more Irish, with a big dose of Scottish; after all her last name will be Stewart.

All right, I guess we can wait until the '60s to try some Asian fusion—I really want to mix colors and races—the best is yet to come!

Stop whining; we need to get to work. This GIRL is supposed to be delivered today, 3 October 1938, at four o'clock in the afternoon! The work order says her parents will go for a walk and she is supposed to arrive in such a hurry that she will make her grand entrance on her Grandmother Stewart's dining room table, on which a newly baked angel food cake is cooling!

Oh goodness, how these drama queens need to make a grand entrance! Okay, get busy! Let's assemble Carole Elaine Stewart and send her on her way.

I have no memory of being assembled, but I can imagine some of the choices. The workers make fun when they throw me together: Hey, did you hear the one about every time an angel sneezes a human gets a cold! Ha HA! Her last name is going to start with an S. We still have some of those discontinued curved spines to get rid of—shall we give her one? A little artistic license about symmetry that she will never get!

I'm tired of doing low hairlines. I think I will put her head of hair on backwards so she can have a high forehead! And green eyes, so they won't compete with the cornflower blue eyes we gave her mother years ago. Good! I will make her very white skinned so she can scare people when she feels like it. Oh what a hoot, I just mixed up the toe sequence so two of her toes are longer than her great toe. Good luck, little lady, finding shoes!

She needs the gift of gab to honor her Irish blood, a scoop of brooding for her Scot's blood, and for the Bavarian bits a wild sense of humor. AND WE ARE DONE!

She will be born under the Star of Libra, with a rising Capricorn and descending Gemini. "I get it: She will be an oversexed peacemaker looking for her twin!!"

Okay enough of the jokes. It's time to drop her into the birthing tube to Planet Earth, ground zero, Pomeroy, Ohio, USA, EST. 4 P.M.

Happy landing, little lady, and may your life be filled with fun and the fireworks. See you later in the recycling bin. Till then, little air symbol, fly away. Cheerio, Guten Tag, Farewell!!

October Anniversary

Today is my birthday and brings me full circle from my first cupcake, "My Arrival." Whenever the slot machine of my life brings up the eights I know I have lived yet another decade. As I have lived the chapters of my life, I realize that every decade has been clearly defined and uniquely different from the last. I hardly recognize some of the Me's I have been. Circumstances, opportunities, and fate certainly do create some amazing scenarios.

A friend once described her life as a movie in which she alone stars. I suppose she is right, and the same could be said for everyone. Comedy, tragedy, the mundane, adrenaline highs, crossroads, loves, and losses we cannot escape. It is how we interpret these roles given by the great casting director of the universe that ultimately creates the indelible unique "me-ness" of us all.

I have accepted my many imperfections and regret that I have caused pain to others whom I love. I do take responsibility for my faults, my chips and cracks that are permanently part of me. I thank my mother for teaching me to stay, by choice, on the sunny side of life. Having hope and believing in goodness brings forth great rewards. I have seen others choose the glass half empty, and knew I didn't belong in that club.

I am sure all the Oktoberfests around the world are in honor of me! Why not? I thank Mother Nature for making the fall so lovely just to please my need for beauty. The arts are my oxygen; my family and friends my soul food. I can't imagine living without laughing, singing, and dancing to the changing rhythms of life.

I now turn the fate of *This Life and the Fireworks* over to you. Meanwhile, may the fireworks of your life bring good fortune to you as they clearly have done for me.

Carole Elaine Stewart Dale

Four O'clock Flower

How do you know when to pull your petals over your face?

How do you know that you will awake with the next day's light?

How do you grow lush green leaves with little blossoms the size of cat eyes out of soil made of poison?

How is it you are strong enough to rise above this fetid field and give grace to a chemical city with sulfurous acid infested smoke instead of air?

How do you endure the coke dust on your face?

You remain a flower for your own reasons.

I watch you all summer and I learn.

Neither DuPont plant's red, green, or mad-dog foam from the Kanawha River can hurt me.

I will survive black lungs and chronic breathing sickness.

Like you I too will flower. No toxic cocktail will tip my scales.

Sometimes I hide in your foliage, and as the filtered sun sets I hear my mother's voice from the house saying how bad I have been that day.

I await safe in your camouflage to be missed.

As darkness falls the call, "Carole, where are you? Time to come in!" does not come.

As I feel the cool dew that will refresh you in the moonlight, I slip out into the darkness and stealthily open the front door and go to my room.

I too will again bloom tomorrow, a flower wild.

Cupcake: Fire as Metaphor

My son Robby, Columbus City Fireman.

Cupcake: Fire as Metaphor

My brother Scotty, soon to leave for Vietnam.

Cupcake: My Arrival

My Mother, Edith Mae, on her Wedding Day.

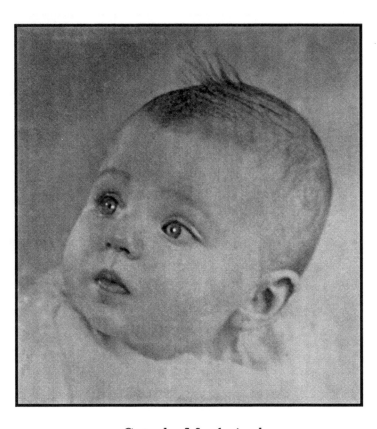

Cupcake: My Arrival

My baby picture.

Cupcake: Life's Lottery

Great Grandparents Jacob and Maria Fischer, and my Grandfather Theodore as a boy.

Cupcake: The Dream

Pomeroy clan at Cave Street house.with Mom. Uncle Dick, Uncle Carl, Mom, Aunt Freda, Aunt Millie, Aunt Marcella, my mother Edith Mae, and Aunt Teddy.

Cupcake: Cute Tomato Lipstick

Scotty and me.

Cupcake: Sleeping in My Bed

My parents with baby brother Scotty and me.

Cupcake: After the Ball

Carole at the Ball.

Cupcake: I Hate Santa Claus

Robby with his cousin Johanna.

Cupcake: California Dreaming

Cable Car San Francisco, me (Elaine) and Carol.

Cupcake: Come Home Right Now!

Aunt Millie

A sample of forthcoming cupcakes:

Rob and I in a Volkswagen caught in tornado winds --
the car lifts off....

The Taj Mahal and King Hussein of Jordon at sunset....

The crow kept calling from
Aunt Millie's bedroom window...

The plane crashes into the...it is my first flight.....

Don't worry; you look GREAT from the front!

When the crows come cawing and I look out into the trees
I know them -- they are my departed family. They have
come to remind me I am one of them and they have not
forgotten me. They, we, are a wild noisy clan and my heart
leaps with pleasure when I hear their sharp caws pierce the
air. The raven is my Native American symbol and crows
are part of my kin. This affinity I have for crows brings me
great pleasure. I believe if we are open to the intangible
mysteries of life, many good spirits can surround us.
Until we meet next on another page, may
the spirits of goodness surround you.

Bye Bye

--or should I say:

Caw Caw!

Carole!

Printed in the United States
151662LV00001B/1/P

9 781438 995632